PENGUIN PLAYS
PL25

I'M TALKING ABOUT JERUSALEM

ARNOLD WESKER

I'm Talking about Jerusalem

ARNOLD WESKER

PENGUIN BOOKS

Penguin Books Ltd, Harmondsworth, Middlesex
U.S.A.: Penguin Books Inc., 3300 Clipper Mill Road, Baltimore 11, Md
AUSTRALIA: Penguin Books Pty Ltd, 762 Whitehorse Road,
Mitcham, Victoria

—

First published 1960

—

For
Della and Ralph

All performing rights of this play are fully protected,
and permission to perform it, whether by amateurs
or professionals, must be obtained in advance from
Theatrework (London) Limited, 12 Abingdon Road,
London, w8, who can furnish all particulars.

Made and printed in Great Britain
by Cox & Wyman Ltd,
London, Reading, and Fakenham

CONTENTS

INTRODUCTION

Every modern epoch seems to produce a small number of artists whose work provides society with an antidote to the awareness of its own exhaustion.

One thinks of men like Grosz and Tucholsky in Germany after the first world war, like Sartre and Camus in France after the second.

In Britain today, it is the New Playwrights who offer this therapeutic service to an ailing body. Of these writers for the theatre, Arnold Wesker may not be the one whose work will have the most lasting fame; he is certainly the one with the most immediately prophylactic effect on his audiences.

Wesker is a romantic, whose romanticism transmutes even disillusionment into an act of affirmation. His plays shame us into admitting the loss of emotion and the abdication from individual responsibility, that defile the age in which we live.

In the third play of his Kahn trilogy, *I'm Talking about Jerusalem*, Wesker traces the efforts of Ada Kahn and her husband Dave Simmonds to build their own Jerusalem, to live a life of human dignity, an existence of Socialism-in-Action rather than Socialism-in-Argument in a Norfolk cottage.

They fail. And Wesker has the honesty – which is the honesty of innocence – to admit that their failure is not caused only by the debased values of a hostile society, debauched by materialism and its by-product cynicism, but also by inherent weaknesses in their own character.

It is this innocence, rather than his political fervour, which helps us to find the key to Wesker's work up to now: the innocence that permits a gift for primitive lyricism full rein, the innocence that allows him to mine his plays out of the seam of personal experience without recourse to the brake of inhibition.

A less innocent, more sophisticated writer, one more acutely conscious of the neuroses that impel an artist to express himself, might well have flinched from making the overt statements of the heart that illuminate all three plays in the trilogy. I am thinking of Beatie Bryant's liberated outburst that brings *Roots* to a close, and, in *I'm Talking about Jerusalem*, Dave and Ada's re-enactment of Genesis for the enlightenment of the child, and Dave's reluctant 'explanation' of his point of view in Act 2:

'I know the city, Sarah. Believe me sweetheart! Since being demobbed I've worked in a factory turning out doors and window frames and I've seen men hating themselves while they were doing it. Morning after morning they've come in with cold hatred in their eyes, brutalized! All their humanity gone. These you call men? All their life they're going to drain their energy into something that will give them nothing in return. . . . That barn'll be my workshop. There I shall work and here, ten yards from me, where I can see and hear them, will be my family. And they will share in my work, and I shall share in their lives. I don't want to be married to strangers. I've seen the city make strangers of husbands and wives, but not me, not me and my wife.'

This kind of verbal ardour is rare on the English stage. It represents an individual artist's *cri de cœur* in the philistine wilderness. Apart from John Osborne – whose *Look Back in Anger* inspired Wesker, by his own admission, to embark on his first full-length play (*Chicken Soup with Barley*) – modern English writers tend to shy away from using the stage for direct autobiographical expression. (They usually prefer the medium of the novel.)

One has to go back to Strindberg and Toller to discover a parallel faith in personal experience as the raw material for didactic dramaturgy.

Yet though he writes in innocence, Wesker is not blind to the playwright's need to state the other side, if only to use the views of its representatives as tools on which his romantic heroes can, to use Wesker's own phrase, 'sharpen their brains'.

Introducing the disenchanted Libby Dobson into *Jerusalem*, Wesker cogently argues the case of the cynic, thereby demonstrating his hitherto underrated quality of craftsmanship. It is in this scene, and in the course of the equally incisive (and fairly conceived) apologia of the materialistic Aunt Esther in the play's final act, that the playwright shows of what he may be capable when the autobiographical material has been written out of his system: the nostalgia for a Jewish community life, the fervent growing-pains of a young Socialist who regards the expediencies of politicians as a personal insult, the strident affirmations of the young writer realizing for the first time that he possesses a voice that can make itself heard.

In *Jerusalem*, the weaknesses of a playwright, whose attitudes are perhaps prematurely inflexible, are still apparent. It is the loosest frame of a most affecting triptych.

In *Chicken Soup with Barley*, the saga of the East End Kahn family observed through the various phases of their political disabusement, the character of Ronnie Kahn (the voice of Wesker himself) is used as the play's protagonist. The things that happen in the play happen to

Ronnie. The boy's political world is made by Spain, broken by Hungary, rebuilt by the indestructible faith of his mother.

In *Roots*, Ronnie reappears as the antagonist, who, never seen by the audience, 'gives words' to the girl 'who could have been a poem' in the act of renouncing his relationship with her.

But in *Jerusalem* Ronnie is not a character essential to the play's dramatic development. He appears from time to time, playing the chorus to the struggle of the two main characters, who give the play its theme and substance.

This is a pedantic point, and at this stage Wesker's work cannot be subjected to, or belittled by, pedantic analysis. It should be recognized for what it is, an authentic voice of our time, which moves us because it echoes, without blur, the conscious unfulfilment of a generation.

Thousands of theatregoers, who are not sufficiently numbed to experience the act of affirmation as an embarrassment, have found in Wesker's trilogy an accurate, valid, even beautiful testament.

Whatever is to follow, this pleasure cannot be diminished.

ROBERT MULLER

CHARACTERS OF THE PLAY AND ORIGINAL CAST

—

First presented at the Belgrade Theatre, Coventry, 28 March 1960, produced by JOHN DEXTER

—

RONNIE KAHN	GEORGE TENSOTTI
ADA SIMMONDS, *his sister*	CHERRY MORRIS
SARAH KAHN, *their mother*	LALA LLOYD
DAVE SIMMONDS, *Ada's husband*	ALAN HOWARD
1ST REMOVAL MAN	KENTON MOORE
2ND REMOVAL MAN	ROBIN PARKINSON
LIBBY DOBSON, *wartime friend of Dave*	
	PATRICK O'CONNELL
COLONEL DEWHURST, *Dave's employer*	PAUL KERMACK
SAMMY, *Dave's apprentice*	KEITH CRANE
DANNY SIMMONDS	PETER PALMER
ESTHER KAHN } *aunts of*	ANN ROBSON
CISSIE KAHN } *Ronnie and Ada*	ROSEMARY LEACH
POSTMAN	REX DOYLE

*

ACT ONE
September 1946

ACT TWO
Scene 1: July 1947
Scene 2: Autumn 1953

ACT THREE
Scene 1: Autumn 1956
Scene 2: 1959

ACT ONE

Norfolk. A house in the middle of fields. We see the large kitchen of the house, the garden, and the end part of an old barn.

September 1946. DAVE *and* ADA SIMMONDS *are just moving in. Boxes and cases are strewn around.* DAVE *and two* REMOVAL MEN *are manoeuvring a large wardrobe, 1930 type, from a lorry off stage.* ADA *is unpacking one of the cases.* SARAH KAHN, *her mother, is buttering some bread on a table, and from a portable radio comes a stirring part of Beethoven's Ninth Symphony.* RONNIE KAHN, *Ada's brother, is standing on a box conducting both the music and the movement of people back and forth.* DAVE *– unlike* ADA *and* RONNIE *– speaks with a slight cockney accent.*

RONNIE: Gently now. Don't rush it. You're winning.

DAVE: Instead of standing there and giving orders why don't you give a bloody hand?

RONNIE: You don't need any more hands. I'm organizing you, I'm inspiring you.

DAVE: Jesus Christ it's heavy, it's heavy. Drop it a minute.

RONNIE: Lower it gently – mind the edges, it's a work of art.

DAVE: I'll work of art you. And turn that radio off – I can cope with Beethoven but not both of you.

RONNIE (*turns off radio*): What are you grumbling for? I've been shlapping things to and fro up till now, haven't I? Only as it's the last piece I thought I'd exercise my talents as a foreman. Don't I make a good foreman? (*Calling*) Hey, Mother, don't I make a good foreman?

SARAH (*coming from the kitchen*): What've you lost?

RONNIE: Listen to her! What've you lost! She's just like her daughter, she can't hear a thing straight. Watch this. Hey, Ada! The sea's not far away you know.

ADA: You can't have any because I haven't put the kettle on yet.

RONNIE: Lunatic family.

DAVE: Come on. We'll never get done. Ready?

(*They bend to lift the wardrobe.* SARAH *returns to kitchen.*)

RONNIE: Heave – slowly – don't strain – heave.

1ST R.M.: Where's it going?

DAVE: Through the kitchen and upstairs.

RONNIE: You won't get through the kitchen, go round the back.

DAVE: We'll manage.

(RONNIE *goes on ahead and pushes* ADA, *the box, and* SARAH *and table out of their path.*)

RONNIE: Make way, make way – the army is marching on its stomach. (DAVE *and the two men are bent forward in effort.*) You see, I can't help, there's not enough room for four to get round that door.

(*They stop at the other end of the kitchen and lower the wardrobe.*)

DAVE: We have to get round here and along the passage.

2ND R.M.: Never. You can't bend wardrobes.

1ST R.M.: Could saw it in half.

RONNIE (*pretending to be offended*): Good God man! An original twentieth-century piece and you want to saw it in half? Ahhhhhhhhh. (*Weeps upon it.*)

1ST R.M.: You still at school?

RONNIE: So?

1ST R.M.: Talk a lot don't you.

RONNIE: What's that got to do with school?

1ST R.M.: Should've thought they'd taught you manners.

SARAH (*coming into battle*): Don't you think he's got manners then?

2ND R.M.: But he talks so don't he?

ADA (*joining battle*): Sooner he talked than he remained silent.

RONNIE: My lunatic family comes to my rescue.

1ST R.M.: I'd've clipped him round the ear if he'd've called me lunatic.

DAVE: We'll have to take it back and use the front entrance.

RONNIE: What's the good of me being a foreman if you don't listen to me.

(RONNIE *again pushes back table and box which women had returned.*)

RONNIE: Make way, make way. The retreat! (*Opens radio again and conducts them and symphony out of kitchen.*)

SARAH: Everything he makes into a joke.

(*The men raise the wardrobe and struggle back, this time going round the back of the house.* RONNIE *pauses and surveys the scene.*)

RONNIE: Nineteen forty-six! The war is really over isn't it, eh, Mother? Aren't you proud that your children are the first to pick up the ruins?

SARAH: I'm proud, yes! (*Pushes radio lid closed.*)

RONNIE: Of course proud! We just put a Labour Party in power didn't we? It's right they should be the pioneers – good! Ever-y-bo-dy is building. Out go the slums, whist! And the National Health Service comes in. The millennium's come and you're still grumbling. What's the matter, you don't like strawberries and cream?

SARAH (*looking around*): Strawberries and cream?

RONNIE: All right, so it's shmultz herring and plum pudding for the meanwhile. But it's a great saga you're witnessing. The wandering Jews strike again! None of the easy life for them, none of the comforts of electricity –

SARAH: They're madmen!

RONNIE: They don't need roads, give them a muddy lane –

SARAH: Tell me Ada, how are you going to get to the village? Not even a road here there isn't. Just fields – a house in the middle of nowhere.

ADA: Ronnie, go and get some water for tea.

RONNIE: And none of the joys of running water for these brave people, a well! A biblical well. I can see you Ada, like Miriam at the well, and Dave will come like Moses and

13

drive away the strangers and draw water for you and you shall love him and marry him, and you shall bear him a son and he will be called Adam and the son shall grow strong and the land of Israel shall grow mighty around him –

SARAH: Yes, here!

(SARAH *moves to throw something on a dustheap out of hearing.*)

ADA: It was Zipporah and Moses anyway.

RONNIE: Zipporah. What a beautiful name. I've always wanted to write the Bible. Ada, haven't you ever felt you've wanted to sit down and write something that's already written? God, how many times I've felt like composing the 'Autumn Journal'.

(SARAH *returns in time to hear this.*)

ADA: What?

RONNIE: You know – Louis MacNeice –

> Sleep, my past and all my sins,
> In distant snow or dried roses
> Under the moon for night's cocoon will open
> When day begins.

ADA: I know what you mean.

SARAH (*surprised*): It's wonderful, Ronnie.

RONNIE: Isn't it beautiful Mother? It's a poetry I can talk, I don't have to recite it.

(*As if telling her something.*)

> Sleep to the noises of running water
> Tomorrow to be crossed, however deep;
> This is no river of the dead or Lethe,
> Tonight we sleep
> On the banks of the Rubicon – the die is cast;
> There will be time to audit
> The accounts later, there will be sunlight later
> And the equation will come out at last.

My God, I want to write it again and again.

SARAH: But Ronnie, you've never read me that one before. Now that one, *that* one you try and get published.

(*At this,* ADA *and* RONNIE *break into uncontrollable laughter.* SARAH *cannot understand why.*)

SARAH: So what's funny?

RONNIE: Oh, Mother I love you, love you. (*He cuddles her.*)

SARAH (*pushing him away because he tends to smother her*): All right so you love me, love me, but what's funny?

RONNIE (*picking up pail and going to get water*): My mother encourages me – get it published she says! (*Goes off laughing.*)

SARAH: Is he gone mad or something?

ADA: Oh, Mummy, you are funny – he was quoting a poem by a famous poet.

SARAH: How did I get such clever children?

RONNIE (*off*): Hey, Ada! How do I get the water out of this well?

ADA (*shouting*): Lift up the lid and hook the bucket on and just let it down.

RONNIE (*after a second*): Hey Ada! There's no water in this well.

ADA (*shouting*): Of course there is, you idiot.

RONNIE: But I can't see it.

ADA: It's a long way down.

RONNIE: You can die of thirst before you get to the bottom.

SARAH (*sighing*): Ada, Ada. You're both mad.

ADA: Next time you come down, we'll have lots of improvements.

SARAH: I don't understand it, I just don't see why you have to come out here. Is London so bad? Millions of people live there!

ADA: Thank you.

SARAH: All of a sudden they pick up and go away.

ADA (*calling*): Dave, where's the paraffin?

DAVE (*off*): I put it in the corner.

ADA: I see it. (*Picks up paraffin and proceeds to fill and light primus stove.*)

SARAH: A primus stove! What's the point? All this heavy work. No roads, no electricity, no running water, no proper lavatory. It's the Middle Ages. Tell me why you want to go back to the Middle Ages?

ADA: We'll get a calor gas stove in time.

SARAH: Progress!

ADA: Mummy, please, ple-ease help us. It's not easy this move, for any of us. Doesn't it occur to you that we desperately need your blessing, please –

SARAH: I'm here aren't I? Silly girl. But how can I bless –? I brought up two nice children, and I want to see them round me – that's wrong? But all right, so you want to go away, so you want to build a life of your own, but here? Why here? Explain it to me, maybe I'll be happier. Why here?

RONNIE (*off, shouting*): Hey, Dave – how you managing?

DAVE (*off*): We're managing. Just a few more stairs.

RONNIE: That's right boys – heave, heave!

DAVE: I'll heave this bloody thing on top of your head if you don't shut up. Go away and make some tea.

RONNIE (*entering*): The men want tea. Feed the workers. Hey Addie – you know what I discovered by the well? You can shout! It's marvellous. You can shout and no one can hear you.

ADA (*triumphantly*): Of course!

SARAH (*derisively*): Of course.

RONNIE: Of course – listen. (*Goes into garden and stands on a tea chest and shouts.*) *Down with capitalism! Long live the workers' revolution!* You see? *And long live Ronnie Kahn too!* (*Waits for a reply.*) No one argues with you. No one says anything. Freedom! You can jump about. (*Jumps off chest.*) You can spin in the air. (*Jumps and spins with arms akimbo.*) You can do somersaults . . . (*He rolls on the grass shouting 'wheeeee'.*) You can bang the earth. (*He thumps the ground with his fists with utter joy.*) My God – it's wonderful – you can go mad all on your own and no one'll say anything. (*Sits up wide-eyed.*)

SARAH: He's not my son. I'll swear he's not my son.

RONNIE (*crawling on all fours up to the kitchen door*): Of course I'm not your son. My real mother was a gipsy and lived in a caravan, and one day she came to your door and instead of buying flowers from her you bought me. And everyone believed us. They used to look at you, and then at me and say no – no, it's true, he doesn't look like you does he?

SARAH: Make the tea.

RONNIE (*springing up*): Where's the kettle?

ADA: In one of the boxes.

RONNIE: It's like camping.

SARAH: Camping!

ADA: Finished the bread Mummy?

SARAH: I've finished the bread. What about the soup?

ADA: Soup?

RONNIE: She made a chicken soup last night and put it in bottles. She puts everything in bottles. (*Looks in Sarah's bag.*)

SARAH: And a meat pie too I made.

ADA: Oh Mummy, you shouldn't have.

SARAH: I shouldn't have, I shouldn't have! Everything I shouldn't have. Did *you* think about what you were going to eat when you came here?

ADA: I brought bread and tomatoes and fruit and cheese.

RONNIE: Cheese!

SARAH: As if I didn't know what you'd bring!

RONNIE: She always offers me cheese when I'm hungry.

ADA: You're both mad.

SARAH: *We're* mad! My children and they still don't know how to organize their lives.

RONNIE (*holding up jar*): Bottled Chicken Soup. It looks like – er – hum – yes, well, I hope it tastes different.

ADA: We've only one primus so you'll have to wait until the water's boiled. Get out a table-cloth Ronnie.

RONNIE: A table-cloth? What, here? Now?

ADA: This place may be a shambles but I don't intend living as though it's one.

(DAVE *and the* REMOVAL MEN *have returned by this time and* RONNIE *throws out a cloth assisted by* SARAH.)

1ST R.M. : Got a problem living here haven't you?

2ND R.M.: Ain't very modern is it, Jim?

RONNIE: Got the wardrobe in place?

2ND R.M.: We got it through the door.

DAVE: You can help me manoeuvre it later, Ronnie.

1ST R.M.: What made you move here, mate? Not being nosey or anything, but you can't say it's everybody's choice of a new home.

DAVE: It's a long story.

2ND R.M.: Couldn't you find a better place? More convenience? I mean it's not very sanitary, is it?

DAVE: Not easy to find the right place with little cash. Saw the job advertised, a cheap house for sale near by – grabbed it!

SARAH: Hard! Everything has to be hard for them.

1ST R.M.: Still, they're young, missus, ain't they? Gotta admit it's fresh out here.

2ND R.M.: Too bleedin' fresh if you ask me.

RONNIE: Come on, Dave. Give them an answer. It's a golden opportunity this. The world has asked you why you've come here. There stands the world (*to* R. MEN) and here stand you two. You're on trial comrade.

ADA: Don't arse around Ronnie, the men want their tea.

RONNIE: But I'm serious, girl. I want to know too. You've

always been my heroes, now you've changed course. You've left communism behind – what now?

1ST R.M.: Communist, are you?

2ND R.M.: That's a dirty word, ain't it?

1ST R.M.: Not during the war it wasn't.

RONNIE: The world is waiting, Dave.

DAVE: I'm not going to make speeches, Ronnie.

SARAH: Is a reason a speech?

DAVE: You can't talk about reasons, Sarah, just like that. A decision grows, slowly – you discover it.

RONNIE: But where did this one start?

ADA: Ceylon.

DAVE: – When I was stationed out there. I was with Air Sea Rescue, boat building.

1ST R.M.: We was in India. That's where Ted and me met. Decided on this game out there.

DAVE: I was in India for a bit. Where were you?

2ND R.M.: Bombay.

DAVE: Karachi, me. That's where I met Libby Dobson, Ada – remember? I always wrote to you about Libby Dobson? Me and him were going to do everything together when we got back to Civvy Street. Like you two. But *that* was a ship in the night.

ADA: He made a great impression on you, though.

DAVE: Taught me a lot. When we get straight we'll have him down here – shouldn't be difficult to trace him. He always wanted to do something like this with me. This'll please him this move, old Libby Dobson'd get a kick out of coming here.

1ST R.M.: What was Ceylon like?

DAVE: Beautiful island. Being a carpenter I used to watch the local carpenters at work. They used to make their own tools and sometimes they'd show me. They'd sit out on the beach fashioning the boats or outside their houses planing and chiselling away at their timber, and they let me sit with them once they knew I was also building boats. And you know, one day, as I watched, I made a discovery – the kind of discovery you discover two or three times in a lifetime. I discovered an old truth: that a man is made to work and that when he works he's giving away something of himself, something very precious –

2ND R.M.: We didn't see anything precious about living in mud huts and working in disease.

DAVE: No, no. You miss the point – I'm talking about the *way* they worked, not the conditions. I know about disease, I know about the mud huts, but what I was trying to say –

ADA: It's no good trying to explain. We're here and let's –

SARAH (*angrily*): Ada stop it! Stop it! Impatience! What's the matter with you all of a sudden. Don't explain! Nothing she wants to explain. No more talking. Just a cold, English you-go-your-way-and-I'll-go-mine! Why?

ADA: Because language isn't any use! Because we talk about one thing and you hear another that's why.

RONNIE: Come on, Dave, you haven't said enough. The world doesn't believe you –

ADA: The world!

RONNIE: Explain more.

ADA: Explain what? We've moved house, what's there to explain? What's so exceptional?

SARAH (*posing the real question*): What's wrong with socialism that you have to run to an ivory tower?

DAVE: Nothing's wrong with socialism Sarah, only we want to live it – not talk about it.

SARAH: Live it? Here?

ADA: Oh the city is paradise I suppose!

SARAH: The city is human beings. What's socialism without human beings tell me?

DAVE: I know the city Sarah. Believe me sweetheart! Since being demobbed I've worked in a factory turning out doors and window frames and I've seen men hating themselves while they were doing it. Morning after morning they've come in with a cold hatred in their eyes, brutalized! All their humanity gone. These you call men? All their life they're going to drain their energy into something that will give them nothing in return. Why do you think these two (*the* R.M.*s*) decided to set up on their own? Eh? I'll tell you –

SARAH: But this isn't a socialist society yet –

ADA: What the hell difference do you think that'll make? All anyone talks about is taking over capitalist society, but no one talks about really changing it.

2ND R.M.: And you're going to change it?

1ST R.M.: On your own, cock?

DAVE: No of course we can't change it. But you see that barn out there? I'll work as a chippy on the Colonel's farm here for a year and then in a year's time that barn'll be my workshop. There I shall work and here, ten yards from me, where I can see and hear them, will be my family. And they will share in my work and I shall share in their lives. I don't want to be married to strangers. I've seen the city make strangers of husbands and wives, but not me, not me and my wife.

SARAH: Words, words.

ADA: *Not* words. At last something more than just words.
(*Pause. Their defiance sinks in.*)

RONNIE (*to* R.M.*s*): So now *you* (*to* ADA *and* DAVE) and now the *world* knows. And the world – will watch you.

1ST R.M.: Come on China. It's time to set off. These socialists can't even make us a cup of tea.
(*At which point the whole Kahn family swing into action with regrets and apologies and thrust sandwiches and fruit into the arms of the startled lorry drivers.*)

2ND R.M.: Oi, oi! Whoa! Merry Christmas!

1ST R.M.: Think of us poor city sods won't you? Good luck!
(*The* R.M.*s go off to the lorry. We hear the lorry start, it revs and slowly moves off in gear. The family stands and watches, and waves and calls 'Goodbye,' listening till the sound dies away.*
Silence.
Each feels that with the going of the lorry has gone the last of the old life.
It is getting dark.)

RONNIE: Well – you're here. You've come. Welcome to the Shambles.
(DAVE *moves to* ADA *and kisses her.* RONNIE *watches.*
SARAH *sits unhappily in a chair away from them all.*)

DAVE: We've got a house.

ADA: We've got a house.

DAVE: Tired darling?

ADA: A bit.

DAVE: It's not *such* a mess.

ADA: I know.

DAVE: It looks it but it's not such a mess.

ADA: I know, angel.

DAVE: Are you in control?

ADA: I'm in control.

DAVE: I love you very much.

ADA: I love you very much.

RONNIE (*moving to* SARAH): And I love you too sweetheart. (*His arm round her*) Look at my sister – (*with mock passion*) isn't she beautiful?

SARAH: I don't understand what went wrong, I don't understand how she can be like that.

ADA (*breaking away from* DAVE): I'm not like anything Mummy, only like your daughter. (*Kisses* SARAH.) You can come and visit us. Look – (*waving arms around with*

22

mock majesty) a country house. Aren't you pleased your daughter's got a country house? We can entertain in grand style! Everyone can come for a holiday – we'll have the maiden aunts down! Aunty Cissie and Aunt Esther can come and pull up weeds for us.

RONNIE: They're really very bourgeois these idealists you know.

SARAH: So far away.

ADA: Only a hundred miles.

SARAH: A hundred miles! You can say it easily. And what if Harry gets worse? It doesn't stop at one stroke, your father's never been very strong.

DAVE: I'm going to unpack some of the things upstairs.

ADA: Light the tilly lamp for me darling before you go up. Supper won't be long. (DAVE *does so.*)

RONNIE: I'm going to look over the district. I bet there are hidden treasures and secret hideouts.

SARAH: Take your raincoat. (RONNIE *does so.*)

DAVE: I suppose *I'll* have to take a candle up with me.

ADA: Come on Mummy. Let's get some supper ready.

SARAH: Do you have to work any more Dave? Can't you rest a little?

DAVE: I'll prepare some beds and take out some of the clothes and hang them. We'll get straight bit by bit. No sense in rushing it. They're good things these lamps. There! It's alight. (*A soft glow covers part of the kitchen.*)

ADA: A lovely light.

SARAH: It took someone all this time to discover electricity – he shouldn't have bothered!

> (DAVE *smiles, shakes his head and goes off upstairs. The women busy themselves. They tidy the general mess and then lay plates and knives and forks on the table.* ADA'S *movements are slow and calm.* SARAH *is volatile and urgent, though somehow she manages to speak slowly and with deliberation – softly. The atmosphere sinks in. Then –*)

SARAH: And Dave doesn't like me – you know that?

(ADA *doesn't reply. Silence. They continue moving around.*)

SARAH: I don't know why it should be that he doesn't like me. I don't think I've ever done anything to hurt him. (*Pause.*) Perhaps that's why he's taking you away, because he doesn't like me. Who knows!

(*Still* ADA *does not reply – instead she very softly starts humming.*)

SARAH: He's changed you. Dave's changed a lot from the old days, Ada. (*Pause.*) Or perhaps he hasn't, perhaps it's me. Who knows. I know he fought in Spain, he's really a wonderful boy but – Ach! children! You bring them up, you teach them this you teach them that, you do what you think is right and still it's no good. They grow up and they grow away and you're left with – with – ! Where do their madnesses come from? Who knows. *I* don't know why Dave doesn't like me.

(*Still no word from* ADA. *She hums perhaps a little louder.*)

SARAH: What you humming for? Humming! All of a sudden she does this humming when I talk to her. A new madness. Stop it Ada. Stop it! Silly girl.

(*An elderly gentleman appears. He is* COLONEL DEWHURST, *the farmer for whom Dave will be working. He comes from the path and knocks on the kitchen door just as* SARAH *finishes.*)

COLONEL (*as the door is opened to him*): Mrs Simmonds? I'm Colonel Dewhurst.

ADA: Oh hello, come in please, we're still unpacking so forgive –

COLONEL: But I undertand, ma'am, I just thought –

ADA: This is my mother. Mother, Colonel Dewhurst, Dave's employer.

COLONEL (*shaking hands*): How do you do, ma'am. You must be very tired. Come a long way today, haven't you?

ADA (*calling*): Dave! Dave! Colonel Dewhurst.

DAVE: I'm coming down, a second.

ADA: Do sit down please.

COLONEL: I was telling your mother you've come a long way today.

ADA: Yes, we have.

COLONEL: It must seem strange.

SARAH: It seems very strange.

ADA: My mother thinks we're mad Colonel.

COLONEL: To come to the country? A fine life, a fine life.

SARAH: With no sanitation or electricity?

COLONEL: Thousands of places like that, thousands! But it's a large house, fresh air –

SARAH: There are parks in London.

COLONEL: *I* wouldn't change now.

SARAH: Maybe you've got some amenities my children haven't?

COLONEL: But they're young, aren't they? It's good they start off with a struggle, makes them appreciate life –

SARAH (*to* ADA): We brought you up with riches I suppose?

DAVE (*appearing and shaking hands*): Hello Colonel Dewhurst.

COLONEL: I thought I'd drop over and see you were arriving safely.

DAVE: That's very good of you.

COLONEL: It won't take you long to get used to it. It's a bracing life in the country.

DAVE: We're not rushing things. I think we'll manage.

COLONEL: Of course you will, yes, I'm sure. When do you think you'll be able to start – er – you know, when can I expect –

DAVE: Well I hoped you wouldn't mind giving us a few days to settle in and get our bearings.

COLONEL: Yes, well, there's no need to come in tomorrow, I think that'll be all right, yes, that'll be all right. But my foreman is waiting to start some fencing – want to get a few more sows in. He's been waiting a long time for a carpenter. No, no need to come in tomorrow – early start the next day'll do, do perfectly.

DAVE: Thanks.

COLONEL: Yes, well, thought I'd pop over and see you were arriving safely. Come at a good time – we've had some rain but it's gone. Doesn't do to have too much rain.

ADA (*not really knowing the reply*): No it doesn't does it?

COLONEL: Talking of rain, Simmonds, I'd advise you to buy yourself a tank to catch the soft water. Good stuff, that. Save you work, too. Not so much to pull up from the well. Buy one with a tap – easier. Don't drink it, though. Use it for washing and things.

DAVE: Thank you for telling us.

COLONEL: I'll see you right. (*Walks out into the garden.* DAVE *and* ADA *follow to doorway.*) You'll learn lots of things as you go along. (*Looks around.*) Good garden here. Grow your own veges. Apple tree there. Prune it a bit. Sturdy barn too, couple hundred years old. Use it for chickens, build a run inside it. You could do that, couldn't you? Build yourself a chicken run?

DAVE: I expect so. A little bit of intelligence can build you anything.

COLONEL (*suddenly become the employer*): Eight o'clock on Wednesday morning, then, Simmonds. Good night to you both. (*Goes off.*)

(DAVE *and* ADA *stand a second and look at each other.*)

SARAH: That's the man you're working for?

ADA (*to* DAVE): He didn't give you much time to settle in did he?

DAVE: No, he didn't did he?

SARAH: You won't have time to scratch yourself, I'm telling you.

26

ADA: Well perhaps he needs you.

DAVE (*certain*): I'm sure he does. (*Not so certain*) But I reckon he could have given us a couple of days to settle in.

ADA: Yes he could have.

DAVE: We're still rushing –

ADA: Seems like it.

> (*They are disappointed.* SARAH *watches them sadly.*)

SARAH: Oh my children, children! Straight away they want to walk into paradise. Perhaps it's a good thing you should start work so soon, you'll settle in the house gradually and working will get you into a stride, a routine. Always have a routine.

ADA (*brightening at this*): Perhaps Mum is right darling. Perhaps it's better to get stuck in straight away.

DAVE: No moping you mean?

ADA: I mean have no time to think we've done the wrong thing.

DAVE: *You* don't think we've done the wrong thing do you darling.

ADA: No – I do not.

DAVE: I do love you. (*Kisses her briefly.*)

ADA: Come on, let's get this food over with. Where's Ronnie?

SARAH: Looking for hidden treasure.

DAVE: He's what?

SARAH: He's gone out exploring – in the mountains there. (*Waves vaguely.*)

ADA: There aren't any mountains in Norfolk Mother.

SARAH: I'm very surprised.

DAVE: What's that fire there?

> (*They all look at a red glow coming from behind the barn.* DAVE *and* ADA *rush off to one side of the barn.*)

DAVE: I hope the bloody fool hasn't been up to any of his tricks.

> (SARAH *stands looking in the direction they've gone. After a*

few seconds RONNIE *strolls in from the other side of the barn. He walks in a kind of daze, clutching a branch, gazing into space.*)

RONNIE: You can build fires under the night sky.

SARAH: What've you been up to you mad boy?

RONNIE: There's bracken in every hedge and you can make fires with them.

SARAH: Have you set the barn on fire?

RONNIE: It's beautiful.

SARAH: For God's sake stop playing the fool and answer me.

RONNIE (*looking around him*): It's all very beautiful.

(ADA *and* DAVE *appear.*)

ADA: Ronnie, you are a nitwit, you could have set the whole place alight.

RONNIE: Oh no. I know about these things.

SARAH: What did he do! I can't get any sense out of him.

DAVE: It's all right – he made a camp fire, don't panic, nothing's burning. Let's eat.

(*They settle down to eat except* RONNIE, *who for the moment leans against a box, still enraptured.*)

SARAH: He's so mad. I get so angry sometimes. Look at him, in a daze. Take your raincoat off and sit down and eat.

(RONNIE *sits down at the table but doesn't take off his raincoat.*)

ADA: What are you sitting down in your raincoat for?

RONNIE: Somehow I feel, I feel – I . . . (*unable to explain*)

ADA: Yes, yes, but why are you eating with your raincoat on?

SARAH: Another madness! Every so often he gets a madness into his head and you can't shake him out of it. I get so annoyed. Ronnie, take your raincoat off!

DAVE: What are you getting upset for, both of you. The boy wants to eat in his raincoat let him eat in his raincoat.

ADA: He's not normal!

DAVE: All right so he's not normal, why should you worry.

ADA: I do worry. I'm not going to sit at the table with him while he's wearing a raincoat. Ronnie take your raincoat off!

(RONNIE *continues eating.*)

SARAH: I don't know what makes him like this. Ronnie take your raincoat off!

ADA: He's so bloody stubborn. *Ronnie!*

DAVE: You and your mother, you're both the same. Why don't you leave the boy alone. What harm is he doing in a raincoat.

ADA: Because it annoys me that's why! (*to* DAVE) Don't side with him Dave because if you side with him he knows he can get away with it.

(SARAH *rises at this point and goes to a corner of the room where she finds an umbrella.*)

DAVE: Now look at us! Here we are quarrelling among ourselves just because your brother is sitting down at the table wearing a macintosh. Have you ever heard such lunacy? What's your mother up to?

(SARAH *sits at the table and opens the umbrella over her and proceeds to eat. Everyone looks at her in amazement. Suddenly* RONNIE *bursts out laughing, jumps up from the chair, kisses her, and takes off his raincoat.* DAVE *sees what has happened and laughs also. There is great merriment.*)

DAVE: Well if you Kahns aren't the most lunatic family I know.

(*They all begin to eat.* SARAH *twists the umbrella once on her shoulders, sticks her hand out to see if the 'rain' has finished, and then folds up the umbrella and eats.*)

SARAH: Don't I know my children!

DAVE: You're all so much alike, that's why.

(*They eat on in silence for a moment until suddenly* SARAH *gets up from the table and moves quickly out from the kitchen to the garden where she takes a handkerchief from her apron. She weeps a little.* RONNIE *rises and goes to the door.*)

RONNIE: Sarah?

SARAH: It's all right, I'm all right, leave me, go back inside and finish eating.

(RONNIE *returns*.)

RONNIE: Tears again.

ADA: I guessed this might happen. Perhaps she shouldn't have come.

DAVE: Can you blame her darling? Ronnie, sit down and let's finish this food.

RONNIE: I'm not really hungry. (*Half annoyed*) She always makes it seem like the end of the world when she cries.

SARAH (*from the garden*): You know, it reminds me of Hungary, where I was born –

ADA: There, she's better again.

SARAH: There used to be high mountains and a river and a waterfall; my brother Hymie once fell into the river and I saved him. He nearly drowned. The mountains had snow on them.

RONNIE (*calling to her*): But there aren't any mountains or waterfalls here Mother.

SARAH (*after a pause, petulantly*): It still reminds me of Hungary.

ADA: Everything reminds her of Hungary. We were listening to Beethoven the other night and she swore black and blue it was based on a Hungarian folk song.

RONNIE: I'll wash up.

DAVE: Come on, let's finish unpacking.

(RONNIE *takes what remains of the water in the kettle and pours it into a basin, shakes some soap powder into it and begins to wash up.* ADA *and* DAVE *stand by one of the boxes, take out the contents one by one, unwrap them and lay them aside.* SARAH *enters, takes a dishcloth, and begins to wipe up what* RONNIE *washes. As they do this* SARAH *begins to sing a soft melodic Yiddish folk song. She can't remember past the first line.* RONNIE *picks up and reminds her.*

They sing together. RONNIE *indicates to* ADA *to join in, she does so and in turn brings in* DAVE. *The new life has started and some of the old has come with them, and –*)

THE CURTAIN FALLS

ACT TWO

SCENE I

July 1947.

Everything is more in order now. Twelve months have passed and with it their first winter.

A signpost saying 'Y.H.A.' with an arrow, leans against a wall, waiting to be knocked into the ground.

The stage is empty. DAVE *appears singing 'Linden Lea' and carrying a roll of linoleum, which he lays down by the back door. He has just returned from work. At the door he pauses and looks out, surveying the countryside. From a room upstairs,* ADA *calls out.*

ADA: Dave?

DAVE: Yes sweetheart.

ADA: My God, what time is it?

DAVE: About five-fifteen. Is Libby here?

ADA: No, he'll be back soon. I'm just finishing this letter.

DAVE: It's all right, don't rush.

ADA: Dave – when did we arrive here?

DAVE: Roughly twelve months ago.

> (DAVE *stays by door and begins to unbutton his tall boots. After some seconds* ADA *appears. She is pregnant. She greets* DAVE *with a kiss and then he nods his head towards the view. They both gaze at it a while and inhale deeply.*)

ADA: The corn is yellow now.

DAVE: Colours for each season. The children will love it.

ADA: We'll teach the children to look at things won't we Dave? I shall make it into a sort of game for them. Teach them to take notice. (*With mock pomp*) Don't let the world pass you by, I shall tell them – (*breathing deeply*) breathe, I shall say, breathe deeply and fill your lungs and open your eyes. For the sun, I shall say, open your eyes for that laaaarge sun.

DAVE: Not long ago that field was brown. What does Libby say to it all, now he's had a chance to look around? We didn't get much of a chance to talk last night because he arrived so late.

ADA: A very strange fish your friend Libby Dobson. He doesn't quite fit the picture you painted of him does he?

DAVE: No he doesn't does he? What's he been up to all day?

ADA: I packed him up some sandwiches and he went out for a day's walking. God knows where. He stood out here and he looked around and he said 'It's all sky isn't it?' and then he stalked off with a 'see you'.

DAVE: He looked very sad and worn old Libby – never thought he'd end up a – what does he call himself?

ADA: A business consultant.

DAVE: He was a bloody fine mechanic in the RAF.

ADA: You're disappointed aren't you darling?

DAVE: Yes I am – daft, but I am. You know there's always one person you want to show your life to – show what you've done – and I've thought Libby Dobson was the bloke – should've thought he'd've understood. Blimey! the man had a hand in shaping my ideas – people! Well that's people I suppose.

ADA: Maybe he'll be better after a day's walk. Get me some water look or he'll come and nothing'll be ready and then he will be riled.

DAVE: Riled! You're a real Norfolk girl already. (*Holding her*) Let's pretend he's not here and let's go to bed and just lie there.

ADA: Let's get this one over first.

DAVE: We'll leave a note for old Dobson and he can get his own supper.

ADA: Darling the water.

DAVE: He's a big boy – he can look to himself.

ADA: Besides *I'm* – we're – hungry.

DAVE: Water.

    (*He goes off singing 'Linden Lea' and* ADA *goes in to lay a salad.* DAVE *begins to talk to her from the back of the house.*)

DAVE (*off*): Darling we must start making new plans.

ADA: I'm making a salad for supper.

DAVE: What?

ADA: Salad!

DAVE: Plans!

ADA: What?

DAVE: Plans!

ADA: No, salad!

    (DAVE *appears at window to kitchen*).

DAVE: Let's get together – what are *you* talking about?

ADA: I said I'm making a salad for supper.

DAVE: Oh. And I said we must start making new plans. We'll start again. (*Returns to well.*)

ADA (*waits, then calls*): What plans?

DAVE (*off*): I want to build a chicken hut –

ADA: Lovely –

DAVE: And then I want to start laying a concrete floor in the barn so that I can build a proper workshop.

ADA: Have you ever laid a concrete floor before?

DAVE: I hadn't ever made a piece of furniture before had I? You learn. You think about it and you learn. How many more buckets of water do you want for Christ's sake?

ADA: Just fill the copper.

DAVE: But I filled it this morning.

ADA: And I used it this morning.

    (DAVE *enters, puffed out, carrying a bucket of water.*)

ADA: Here, put the spare one in the jug.

    (ADA *draws a jug from under the sink.*)

DAVE: And that's another thing. I've got to take a pipe from the sink to the well and run it into a drain outside.

ADA: A plumber too.

DAVE: And then we must start thinking about buying a soft water tank, that'll save arms at the well.

ADA: Darling, I need storage space. The one cupboard you built there isn't enough.

DAVE: In time my darling, all in good time. We've made our garden grow haven't we? We've made our garden grow and we've stopped our roof from leaking. I've boarded the old stables up and laid by timber ready to work. The rooms are painted white and nearly all the windows have curtains, and in three months' time I reckon I can start on my own. Look, only the hedges are wild. All in good time my darling.

ADA: And Mummy asks us what we do with our time. They're mad.

DAVE: Think we'll stick it out?

ADA: What the hell kind of question is that –

DAVE: Relax Ada – you've gone all tense – you'll give birth to a poker.

ADA: Dave, and that's another thing. I'm worried about the baby. I've been reading that –

DAVE: Whatever you've been reading forget it! Look at you, you're so healthy. Your belly is high and the baby is probably so big that he's bored with it all. (*Puts his ear to her stomach and has a conversation with the baby.*) Listen, he's talking.

ADA: You're mad darling.

DAVE: I tell you he's talking. Yes. Yes, I can hear you – sounds like a dozen drains emptying – what's that? You don't want to come out? But you've got to come out, I don't care how comfortable it is you'll get cramp. No I'm not going to send a bloody taxi for you – you'll walk. Now you listen to me, you come out when you're told or I'll plug you in there for life – you hear me?

ADA: Dave, for God's sake, don't be crude.

DAVE (*snuggling up to her*): Yes, let's be crude.

ADA: In the middle of fields?

DAVE: Right in the middle of fields, one night, at full moon. (*At this moment* LIBBY DOBSON *appears. He's stocky, about 30 years old, and looks as though he wants to be a fisherman and can only be one on holidays.*)

DOBSON: Quite a hideout you've got here, haven't you?

DAVE (*hopefully*): What do you think of it now you've seen it Libby?

DOBSON: You're going to turn it into a youth hostel?

DAVE: Got to make some spare cash somehow mate.

DOBSON: These places really do cater for the hale and bloody hearty, don't they? There – (*puts two bottles on the table*) wine for the table and the whisky's for me. I'm going up to change. (*Goes off.*)

DAVE: Well, I wonder what sort of evening this is going to be?

ADA (*picking up a bucket of waste from under sink and throwing it outside back door*): It'll be all right Dave. People aren't ever as you remember them – you'll just have to get to know each other again.

(*Outside* ADA *notices the rolls of linoleum. Puts down bucket and undoes them.*)

ADA: What's this darling?

DAVE: Some old lino the Colonel threw away. We can use that in the hallway.

ADA: Threw away?

DAVE: Well I saw it lying around in the shed. It's been there for months.

ADA: Did you ask him?

DAVE: But it's been lying around for ages.

ADA: Dave I'm not very moral about taking odd things from employers but I'd hate to have him –

DAVE: It's all right sweetheart I tell you.

ADA: You say it's all right but –

DAVE: Ada, the supper. Libby's hungry and so am I. I want to wash.

(DAVE *pours himself water into bowl and strips to the waist to wash.* ADA *proceeds to lay the table.*)

ADA: Shall I bring out the wine glasses?

DAVE: Bring out the wine glasses.

ADA: Darling don't be cross.

DAVE: But you go on so.

ADA: I don't want things to go wrong.

DAVE: Well a lot will go wrong – so? Are you going to get upset each time?

ADA: Will you light the lamp when you've finished please?

DAVE: I mean a lot *is* going to go wrong isn't it?

ADA: This is different, I–

(DOBSON *returns at this point and sits down, waiting for the next move. Remember, he has already caught them embracing.* DAVE *and* ADA *glance at each other,* DAVE *shrugs his shoulders.* ADA *proceeds to lay out a clean shirt for* DAVE, *he prepares a salad. They never get round to eating it.*)

ADA: Don't forget the lamp when you've done please Dave.

DOBSON: Tilly lamps – the lot. You two have really taken your backward march seriously, eh? Dead serious – cor!

DAVE: Libby – what is it mate, come on, out with it – what's nettled you?

DOBSON: Oh no, Simmonds, please. No old chums and their war memories – I'm on holiday. I'll help you chop your wood – I'll even dance round the may-pole with you – but no heart-searching, I'm a tired man.

(*Throughout an awkward silence the lamp is lit. During this next scene* DOBSON *drinks his whisky, becoming more and more tipsy; just now he stares at the sky.*)

DOBSON: The countryside smells like a cow with diarrhoea.

ADA: Perhaps your nose is still full of smoke and petrol fumes.

DOBSON: Jesus! I could've recognized that remark a mile off.

If I hadn't known, it would have told me your whole story. Our horrible industrial civilization. We hate the large, inhuman cities. Eh? Back to nature, boys.

(*An embarrassed silence.*)

ADA (*to* DAVE): I had a letter from Ronnie today.

DAVE: What does your mad brother say?

ADA: You remember his girl friend Jacqueline? The one he told us knew it all? Well he's come to the dramatic conclusion that people who are similar aren't much good to each other so he's going to marry a prostitute!

DOBSON: Oh God! I bet your mother's in the Salvation Army.

(ADA *and* DAVE *laugh uproariously at this.*)

ADA: Can you imagine Sarah in the Salvation Army? 'Comrades, Jesus Christ was the first communist to be born among us.'

DOBSON: Now the picture is complete. Two ex-communists! There's nothing more pathetic than the laughter of people who have lost their pet faith.

(*The laughter is dead. That was a bomb.*)

DAVE: What the hell *is* the matter with you Libby? Within a few minutes you've called us idealists as if you were swearing at us, and then you express disgust because you think we've lost our faiths.

ADA: Let's have some of your wine shall we?

DOBSON: Yes, let's.

DAVE: You're being offensive Libby.

DOBSON (*wearily*): Oh, come off it! I'm a cynic. You can recognize a cynic, can't you? You should be using me, sharpening your ideas on me. The more sceptical I become the higher your ideals should soar, shouldn't they? Eh? Well, soar then – soar! Be heroic! There's nothing wrong with idealism, only when it's soft and flabby. The smell of petrol in my nose! So what! You can't change the world because it smells of petrol.

ADA: Who's talking about changing the world?

DOBSON: Then go home. Be good children and go home, because you'll never make the beautiful, rustic estate.

ADA: My God darling – it's come to something when we're sneered at for wanting beautiful things.

DOBSON: Because it's a lie. Outdated! Because it's not new!

DAVE: New! New! Everything has to be new! Contemporary! You could walk around on your hands all day – that's new – but it wouldn't be achieving much would it?

DOBSON: That's better – you're bristling, you're bristling. Soon you'll be able to devour me. That's what a cynic's for, Davey mate, to be devoured, gobbled up.

DAVE (*to* ADA): I don't understand it darling. Everyone accuses us of something or other – rustics, escapists, soft-headed. (*To* DOBSON) You think there aren't problems here?

ADA: There isn't a servant to draw our water, you know?

DAVE: Or a gardener to grow our vegetables.

ADA: Do you think I'm going to have a nanny to see to my child?

DAVE: Or that there's a private income somewhere?

ADA: In London you waste your time solving the wrong problems.

DAVE: Leaving early to catch the bus! Is that living?

ADA: But God forbid we should ever imagine that we're changing that world by living here.

DOBSON: Then there's not much point in doing this sort of thing, is there?

DAVE: Not even on an individual level?

DOBSON: What do you mean, 'an individual level'?

DAVE: For God's sake stop asking us what we mean by perfectly simple phrases.

DOBSON: That's just it! They are simple phrases. Simple, inane, and irresponsible! Individual level! Have you ever taken your ideas to their logical conclusion? Well, have you?

Hasn't a worker in a factory ever looked at you as though
you were mad – a little potty, you know? Would you
have the world do without cars, planes, electricity, houses,
roads? Because *that's* the logical conclusion. If no man
should be tied to turning out screws all his life, then that's
what it means. No screws – no transport! No labourers –
no roads! No banks or offices – no commercial market!
No humdrum jobs, then no anything! There you are, solve
it! Go on. Think about it. Reorganize the world so's
everyone's doing a job he enjoys, so everyone's 'expressing'
himself. Go on. Universal happiness? Get it!

DAVE: Now who's being wet? Happiness? (*Mimicking*) What
do you mean by happiness? It's the *doing*, the doing! Do
you think we care that the city was large or smelt of
petrol? It was the boredom, man – the sheer boredom.
Nine to five! Mass production! Remember? It numbed us,
made us soggy and soft. There! *That's* being soggy and
soft! Happiness! My God, you cynics are the soggiest.

DOBSON: Nicely, nicely, Davey. Look, only my head and
arms are left.

ADA: You sound as though you really believe in Jerusalem.

DOBSON: Shrewd girl. Of course I believe in Jerusalem, only
I personally can't measure up to it.

ADA: Because your type always tries to win with words that's
why – but you never *do* anything, you're never at peace
long enough.

DOBSON (*the harshness gone*): The idyll was really broken,
wasn't it? I could see it in your faces. Dave's old blood
brother has sold his soul. But what do you really know
about me, that you think you can say that?

DAVE: We hadn't much of a chance had we comrade? You
weren't exactly inviting were you?

DOBSON: I've tried it, Dave – listen to me and go home –
I've tried it and failed. Socialism? I didn't sell out that

easily. You've gone back to William Morris, but I went back to old Robert Owen. Five thousand pound my old man left me, and I blushed when I heard it. But I still hung on. It's not mine, I decided – the profits of exploitation, I said. Right! Give it back! So I worked out a plan. I found four other young men who were bright mechanics like myself and who were wasting their talents earning ten pounds a week in other men's garages, and I said 'Here's a thousand pounds for each of you – no strings, no loans, it's yours! Now let's open our own garage and exploit no one but ourselves. There's only one provision,' I said, 'only one: as soon as there is an excess profit of another thousand pounds, we find someone else to inherit it and we expand that way!' See the plan? A chain of garages owned and run by the workers themselves, the real thing, and I will build it myself. Can you imagine what a bloody fool they must have thought me? Can you guess the hell of a time they had planning to buy me out? Democracy, mate? I spit it! Benevolent dictatorship for me. You want Jerusalem? Order it with an iron hand – no questions, no speeches for and against – bang! It's there! You don't understand it? You don't want it? Tough luck, comrade – your children will! (*To* ADA) No peace? You're right, Mrs Simmonds. I'm dirtied up. Listen to me, Dave, and go home before you're dirtied up.

ADA: You've nearly finished that whisky Libby.

DOBSON: Is that all you can say? I've just related a modern tragedy and you're warning me against alcohol. She's a real woman this Ada of yours. A woman dirties you up as well, you know. She and the world – they change you, they bruise you, they dirty you up – between them, you'll see.

DAVE: And you call the idealist soft and flabby do you?

ADA: Let's drop it Dave – I think Libby's had enough.

DOBSON: On no, you mean you've had enough. The little

woman senses danger – marvellous instinct for self-preservation. I suppose you two consider you are happily
married for ever and ever and ever. (*Pause.*) I was married
once. God knows how it happened – just after demob. I
used to watch her as the weeks and months went by; I used
to sit and watch fascinated and horrified as – as she
changed. This was before the old man died and we both
went out to work. After supper we'd wash up and she'd
sit by the fire and fall asleep. Just fall asleep – like that.
She might glance at a newspaper or do a bit of knitting,
but nothing else – nothing that might remind me she was
alive. And her face would go red in front of the fire and
she'd droop around and be slovenly. And I just watched
her. She chewed food all the time, you know. Don't
believe me? I watched her! Chewing all the time. Even in
bed, before she went to sleep – an apple or a piece of
gateau – as though terrified she wasn't getting enough
into her for that day. And she became so gross, so undeli-
cate, so unfeeling about everything. All the grace she had
was going, and instead there was flesh growing all around
her. I used to sit and watch it grow. How does one ever
know, for Christ's sake, that a woman carries the seeds of
such disintegration? Then I tried what your brother wants
to do – take a simple girl, a girl from an office, lively un-
cluttered. Wife number two! Just about the time I in-
herited my five thousand pounds. A real socialist enterprise
and a simple wife. Ironic, really. There was I putting a
vision into practice, and there was she watching me in
case I looked at other women – making me feel lecherous
and guilty. She's the kind that dirties you up. There was I
sharing out my wealth and there was she – always
wanting to possess things, terrified of being on her own.
She marries a man in order to have something to attach to
herself, a possession! The man provides a home – bang!

She's got another possession. *Her* furniture, *her* saucepans, *her* kitchen – bang! bang! bang! And then she has a baby – bang again! All possession! And this is the way she grows. She grows and she grows and she grows and she takes from a man all the things she once loved him for – so that no one else can have them. Because, you see, the more she grows, ah! the more she needs to protect herself. Clever? Bloody clever! I think I hate women because they have no vision. Remember that, Davey – they haven't really got vision – only a sense of self-preservation, and you will get smaller and smaller and she will grow and grow and you will be able to explain nothing because everything else will be a foreign language to her. You know? Those innocent I-don't-know-what-you're-talking-about eyes?

DAVE: Make an early night Libby, yes?

(DOBSON *rises, suddenly, furious at being told to go to bed. But his own terrible honesty defies him. He shrinks, looks at them for a sort of forgiveness, and then shrugging his shoulders turns and goes, taking maybe something to chew from the table.*)

ADA: Do you realize he was talking about what I might become darling?

DAVE: Are you worried?

ADA: Do we really appear like that to you men?

DAVE: You *are* worried aren't you?

ADA: I suddenly feel unclean.

DAVE: A cynic works that way darling. Perhaps he's right when he says we should use him, sharpen ourself on him. I don't know what to say – the man's certainly been bruised hasn't he? Does that make him more reliable or less – I never know.

ADA: The futile pursuit of an ideal. Suddenly it all makes me sick. Like eating too many good things.

DAVE: Right! Then enough now. We're not going to be dragged into this discussion again. We are not going to go around apologizing for the way we live. Listen to people and we'll go mad. Enough now!

(*Someone is coming from the lane. A torchlight appears. A voice calls. It is* COLONEL DEWHURST.)

COLONEL: Is anyone at home? Hello there. Simmonds.

ADA: It's Dewhurst. At this hour! (*Opens door to him.*) In here Colonel. Come in.

COLONEL: Good evening.

DAVE: Good evening Colonel Dewhurst. Have a seat. Would you like some wine?

COLONEL: This is not a social visit, Simmonds.

DAVE: That sounds very ominous.

ADA: Do have wine Colonel – it's very good.

COLONEL: Please, Mrs Simmonds. You're making it very difficult for me.

DAVE: Difficult?

COLONEL: I've treated you well, Simmonds, haven't I!

DAVE (*not knowing how it's coming*): Ye-es.

COLONEL: That's right, I have. Helped you when you started. Gave you advice.

DAVE: I'm very grateful Colonel, but –

COLONEL: Well, you don't show it!

DAVE: I'm sorry but I don't know what you're talking about.

COLONEL: The lino, the lino! That's what I'm talking about, and you know that's what I'm talking about. Look, Simmonds, you're an intelligent man – you're not the usual sort who works for me, and I didn't expect you to lie. Still, I didn't expect you to steal from me, but you did. Now don't waste time, just tell me and we'll see what we can do: did you or didn't you take two rolls of lino from the shed near the workshop?

DAVE: Those rolls you threw away and said were no use?

ADA: Dave –

DAVE: Darling – let *me*. No Colonel, I did not.

COLONEL: But I don't understand why you're lying. In fact I don't understand you at all, Simmonds. What did you come to the country for? It's a different way of life here, y'know. They're a slow people, the country people – slow, but sound. I know where I am with them, and they know their place with me. But with you I could never –

DAVE: Never get the right sort of master-servant relationship?

COLONEL: Yes, if you like. But you didn't like, did you? You spoke to me as if I were a – a –

DAVE: An equal.

COLONEL: I don't like it, Simmonds. I'm not a slave driver, but I believe each person has his place.

DAVE: You're decent like, but it's a favour like?

COLONEL: Are you talking to me about decency, Simmonds?

DAVE: You didn't come all the way up that lane just to find out whether I stole two rolls of lino did you Colonel?

ADA: For God's sake Dave –

DAVE: Now Ada!

COLONEL: Yes I did come all the way up that lane, and I'm damn well furious that I had to. Listen Simmonds, I've got to sack you, because by now all my other men know you took the rolls, and they know I know, and if I don't sack you they'll all think they can get away with pilfering. But thinking you were a decent chap, I thought I'd come here and just tell you what a fool you'd been, and discuss what we could do about it. Now I find you're a petty liar and I'm furious, and I don't care what you do. Good night.

DAVE: But you haven't even any proof – I mean –

COLONEL: You must be insane. And what's outside your back door? (*Silence.*) Well, what is it?

DAVE (*weakly*): You said you didn't want it.

COLONEL: Of course I didn't. Junk! Two and sixpence worth of junk – but that isn't the point.

ADA: What is the point Colonel?

COLONEL: You don't really know the point, do you? We 'ask', Simmonds: in my sort of society we ask. That's all. It's twenty-four hours' notice I'm giving, but there is no need to turn up tomorrow. (*He leaves.*)

ADA: You bring the habits of factory life with you? What got into you?

DAVE: Oh God. What a bloody fool I am.

ADA: But I don't understand. Didn't you *know* the lino was outside and that he might see it?

DAVE: I took a chance that it might be dark –

ADA: Oh my God!

DAVE (*surprised*): I feel so ashamed.

ADA: It was so humiliating – if only you'd admitted it –

DAVE: To be caught for something so petty –

ADA: To be doubly caught for lying as well.

DAVE: Jesus! I feel so ashamed.

> (*For some seconds* DAVE *sits, thoroughly crushed.* ADA *is appalled and uncertain what to do.*)

ADA: Well we're not going back to London because of this ridiculous blunder. You're so bloody soft sometimes.

DAVE: Ada I'm sorry.

ADA: You'll have to start your workshop earlier that's all.

DAVE: But we can't afford it.

ADA: Well we'll *have* to afford it. I'm *not* giving up. We'll eat less, we'll buy less, we'll do something but I'm not going away from all this. Thank God the house is still ours anyway. By Christ, Dave – your ideals have got some pretty big leaks in places haven't they?

> (DAVE *is deeply hurt by this and* ADA *realizes she has struck deeply. Perhaps this is the first time she has ever hurt*

46

him so deeply. They wander round the room in silence now, clearing up the table.)

DAVE: Could you *really* see me leaving?

(*More silence – the battle dies in silence and the wounds heal quietly. The meal is being finally set.*)

ADA: I can help mix cement for the workshop floor you know – I've developed big muscles from drawing water up the well.

DAVE (*looks at her gratefully*): Oh God I feel such a fool.

(*Then after a second DAVE lays his hands on ADA's shoulders, takes her to a chair, sits her gently on it, places a stool under her feet, takes an olive branch from out of the pot and, first offering it to her, lays it on her lap. Then he looks around and finds a large red towel which he shrouds on her head and shoulders. Then he steps back and kneels in homage. There he remains for a moment till gently he laughs and gradually ADA laughs too. And on their laughter –*)

THE CURTAIN FALLS

SCENE 2

Late autumn afternoon, 1953. Six years have passed.

The front wall of the barn has been raised, revealing a furniture-maker's workshop.

DAVE *is just stepping out of the barn carrying, triumphantly, a chair that he and* SAMMY *have just made.* SAMMY *is* DAVE's *apprentice.* DAVE *is singing* (*pom-pom*) '*Land of Hope and Glory*' *while* SAMMY *is on his knees applauding and bowing at the spectacle. As* DAVE *majestically lays chair on the 'horse'* SAMMY *speaks. It is fine craftsmanship.*

SAMMY: Looks as though it's sitting down don't it!

DAVE: When a chair does that, it works. (*Pause.*) But there's something wrong with this one.

SAMMY: Shall us have it apart?

DAVE: No, no. Leave it a while. Pour us out another cuppa. We'll look at it. (*Walks round chair.*) The legs are too big.

SAMMY: Hell! Have 'em any smaller and you'll be sitting on the floor.

DAVE: True, true. (*Thinks.*) A wrinkle! A little wrinkle! Old Dave's learnt a lot in six years. Give 'em a slight curf with the saw *in between* the joints. Won't need much. Now then, let's have a little clear up shall we? Get the glue on!

SAMMY: When's he coming to see his chair?

DAVE: Who, Selby? Shortly, shortly.

SAMMY: I don't go much on him you know. He run a seed-sorting factory. Selby's seeds! Old compost! And they reckon he don't pay his men too well neither.

DAVE: Bit fly eh?

SAMMY: Yearp, fly. And he started as a farm labourer hisself look.

DAVE: Well we've agreed on a good price for the chair anyway.

SAMMY: And you mind you stick to it too. I'll sharpen your chisels. (*Does so.*)

DAVE: The boy say anything to you when you took him to school this morning?

SAMMY: He jabbers a lot don't he?

DAVE: He's like all the Kahns. A funny kid. Comes home with the strangest stories. He's a smasher. Misses his mummy though.

SAMMY: What time train is Ada catchin' from London?

DAVE: Left about twelve this morning I think.

SAMMY: You heard from her? She say how her father was?

DAVE: Not well at all, not well at all poor Harry. This is his second stroke and it seems to have knocked him quite hard. (*He is looking at the chair now.*) I don't think I will. I'll leave the seat as it is. Once you start taking off a piece here and there it makes it worse. It's not all that out of proportion. What say you bor?

SAMMY: Well listen to you then! What say you bor! A proper Norfolk article you're talking like.

DAVE: You taking the mickey out of me? (*Throws a handful of shavings over Sammy's head.*) Are you? (*Another.*) Are you? Are you? Eh?

(SAMMY *throws back shavings, at which* DAVE *cries 'War!' and picks up a stick. A fencing duel takes place till* SAMMY *falls defeated.*)

SAMMY: Hey pack it in ole son, Mister what's-his-name'll be here soon to have a look at this here squatting chair of his.

DAVE: Look at this mess you've made. Sweep it up at once. Untidy ole bugger.

(SAMMY *gathers shavings on his hands and knees with brush and pan. He wants to say something to* DAVE, *and is uncertain how to start.*)

SAMMY: Dave, it'll be a while before Ada come won't it?

DAVE: Yes.

SAMMY: I want a little word with you then.

DAVE: Go on son. I'm listening, but I must get this ready for glueing.

SAMMY: I want to leave soon.

DAVE: That was a very short word. Leave?

SAMMY: I aren't satisfied Dave.

DAVE: Satisfied?

SAMMY: Well I don't seem to be getting anywhere then.

DAVE: But you're learning something boy, you're learnin' to do something with your hands.

SAMMY: But nothing a factory can't do just as well as what we do.

DAVE (*shocked*): Have you ever seen inside a factory? You want to stand by a machine all day? By a planer or a sander or a saw bench?

SAMMY: They change around all the time.

DAVE: Excitement! You change machines! Big difference! All your life Sammy, think of it, all your life.

SAMMY: But you get more money for it.

DAVE: That I do not have an answer to. (*Pause.*) Sammy, remember that chair? Remember what you said about it? It looks as though it's sitting down you said. That's poetry boy, poetry! No not poetry, what am I talking about. Er – it's – it's – O Jesus how do you start explaining this thing. Look Sammy, look at this rack you made for your chisels. Not an ordinary rack, not just bits of wood nailed together, but a special one with dove-tail joints here and a mortise and tenon joint there, and look what you put on the side, remember you wanted to decorate it, so you used my carving tools and you worked out a design. For no reason at all you worked out a design on an ordinary chisel rack. But there was a reason really wasn't there? You enjoyed using those tools and making up that design. I can remember watching you – a whole afternoon you spent on it and you used up three pieces of oak before you were satisfied. Twenty-seven and six you owe me.

SAMMY: Hell, that were only messing around.

DAVE: *Not* messing around. Creating! For the sheer enjoyment of it just creating. And what about the fun we had putting up this workshop?

SAMMY: It's not that I don't enjoy myself Dave.

DAVE: But that's not all cocker. It's not only the fun or the work – it's the place. Look at it, the place where we work. The sun reaches us, we get black in the summer. And any time we're fed up we pack up and go swimming. Don't you realize what that means? There's no one climbing on our backs. Free agents Sammy boy, we enjoy our work, we like ourselves.

SAMMY: You think I don't know these things, hell Dave. But I've seen the boys in the village, I know them, they don't care about things and I see them hang around all their lives, with twopence halfpenny between them an' half a dozen dependants. But I want to get on – don't you think I ought to get on?

DAVE: A bait! A trap! Don't take any notice of that clap-trap for God's sake boy. For every hundred that are lured only one makes it. One, only one. Factories? Offices? When you're in those mate you're there for good. Can't you see that? (*No answer.*) No, you can't can you? Of course you can't. Jesus, I must be mad to imagine I could fight everyone. Sammy, I'm sorry mate – I just –

(*At this moment* ADA *appears. She looks pale and weary.*)

DAVE: Ada! Sweetheart! (*He doesn't know who to talk to first.*)

SAMMY: I'm away home to my tea now Dave. See you tomorrow. How are you Ada? (*Retires quickly.*)

DAVE: Sammy, think again boy, we'll talk some more tomorrow, we'll talk tomorrow, you hear?

ADA: What's been happening?

DAVE: He wants to leave. Work in a factory. Ada, how ill you look. (*Goes to embrace her, she takes his kiss but does not respond.*)

ADA: I met Selby in the village.

DAVE: And?

ADA: He wants to cancel the order for the chair.

DAVE: Cancel it? But it's made.

ADA: The price is too high he says.

DAVE: High? But we agreed – the bastard. That's the third person's done this on me. Blast them, all of them. Twentieth-century, short-sighted, insolent, philistine-type bastards! And the world depends upon them, you know that Ada? Oh sweetheart, what an awful welcome.

(*Again he moves toward her but she moves away to sit on a stool.*)

What is it Ada? Why don't you let me touch you all of a sudden, so long and – O my God, it's Harry, idiot I am, I didn't ask, he's not . . .

ADA: No, he's not dead.

DAVE: Then how is he?

ADA: He was raving when I got there.

DAVE: Raving? Old Harry?

ADA: The second stroke affected his brain. He was in a padded cell.

DAVE: O God, Ada –

(DAVE *stretches to her but she continues to refuse his comfort.*)

ADA: He didn't recognize me at first. He was lying on his back. You know how large his eyes are. They couldn't focus on anything. He kept shouting in Yiddish, calling for his mother and his sister Cissie. Mummy told me he was talking about Russia. It seems when they first brought him into the ward he threw everything about – that's why a cell. He looked so frightened and mad, as if he were frightened of his own madness.

DAVE: But what brought it on? I mean don't the doctors know?

ADA: A clot of blood. It's reached the brain. And then he recognized me and he looked at me and I said 'Hello Daddy – it's Ada' and he started screaming in Yiddish 'Dir hust mir, dir hust mir, dir host mirch alle mul ger hust!' You hate me and you've always hated me. (*She breaks down uncontrollably.*) Oh darling I haven't stopped crying and I don't understand it, I don't understand it because it's not true, it's never been true.

(DAVE *holds her tightly as she cries, and smothers her with kisses.*)

DAVE: Hush darling, gently, gently. It was a sick man screaming, a sick man, hush – O good God.

(*They stand a while. Then* ADA *pulls away and starts mechanically unpacking her case.*)

ADA: He smiled and kissed me a lot before I left, it was an uncanny feeling, but you know Dave (*surprised at the thought*) I feel like a murderer.

DAVE: *Ada!* You gone mad? A murderer? Stop this nonsense. You think you were responsible for his illness?

ADA (*calmly*): No, I don't think I was responsible for his illness and neither did I hate him. But perhaps I didn't tell him I loved him. Useless bloody things words are. Ronnie and his bridges! 'Words are bridges' he wrote, 'to get from one place to another.' Wait till he's older and he learns about silences – they span worlds.

DAVE: No one made any rules about it. Sometimes you use bridges. Sometimes you're silent.

ADA: What bridges? Bridges! Do you think I know what words go to make *me*? Do you think I know why I behave the way I behave? Everybody says I'm cold and hard, people want you to cry and gush over them. (*Pause.*) During the war, when you were overseas, I used to spend nights at home with Sarah and the family. There was never a great deal of money coming in and Mummy sometimes got my shopping and did my ironing. Sometimes she used to sit up late with me while I wrote to you in Ceylon, and she used to chatter away and then – fall asleep. She'd sit, in the chair, straight up, and fall asleep. And every time she did that and I looked at her face it was so sweet, so indescribably sweet – that I'd cry. There! Each time she fell asleep I'd cry. But yet I find it difficult to talk to her! So there! Explain it! Use words and explain that to me.

DAVE: What's going to happen to Sarah, Ada? Do you reckon we ought to think about returning?

ADA (*turning to him, slowly and deliberately*): She doesn't need me. Is that hard? She was born to survive every battle that faces her and she doesn't need me. You say I'm like her? You're right. I shall survive every battle that faces me too, and because this place means survival for me we – are – staying – put!

(DAVE *takes her hands and kisses them, then her lips. A child's voice calls:* 'Mummy, Ada, Mummy, Ada, Mummy, Ada!')

DAVE: It's the boy. Watch how pleased he'll be, he kept asking when you were coming. I bet you a dollar the first thing he'll want you to do is play your game with him.

ADA: Danny?

DANNY (*off, assuming a gruff voice*): I'm Daniel the lion killer.

ADA: You're who?

DANNY: I've come to slay your lions for you.

ADA: How much do you charge?

DAVE (*taking out his pipe*): Mothers!

DANNY: I charge sixpence a lion.

ADA: The last time I saw you you were so small, I don't know whether I could trust you to slay my lions.

DANNY: I'm as tall as an elephant.

ADA: I can't possibly believe that. Come out and show yourself Daniel the lion killer.

DANNY: I shan't show myself until you play the game with me.

ADA: Oh! And what is the game today Daniel?

DANNY: It is called 'Look I'm alive!'

(DAVE *does a there-I-told-you-so look.*)

ADA: Oh that one. All right. Are you ready?

DANNY: Yes. Now you do it with me.

(*Now* ADA *faces us and goes through the same actions as we must assume* DANNY *does. She starts crouched down, with her face hidden in her arm – as in the womb.*)

ADA: Are you crouched down?

DANNY (*in his own voice*): Yes Mummy.

(*DAVE pulls a face at her so she draws him into the game too.*)

ADA: Do you mind if my friend here plays Mr Life? (*DAVE tries to run away.*) *Dave!*

DANNY: No, hurry up, I'm getting cramp.

(*What happens from now must have the touch of magic and of clowning. The day has gone and now the light fades slowly into evening.*)

DAVE (*bowing first to ADA, then to DANNY*): I am – (*pauses to ADA*) what's it?

ADA: You're Mr Life.

DAVE: Oh yes, Mr Life. I am Mr Life. I have spent all day making furniture and now I am going to make a human being. You are clay and I am going to make you into a human being. I am going to breathe the fire of life into you. Hissssss, Hissssss, Hissssss.

(*As DAVE breathes the fire ADA unfolds and rises very slowly – this is what DANNY is doing unseen – her eyes are closed.*)

DAVE: Now you have life and you can breathe.

(*ADA breathes deeply.*)

DAVE: Now I will give you sight.

(*He snaps his fingers at DANNY then at ADA. ADA opens her eyes. There is wonder and joy at what is revealed.*)

DAVE: Now I will give you movement.

(*DAVE beckons to DANNY then to ADA. ADA raises and lowers her arms twice, moving her head from left to right at the same time, full of curiosity and excitement at what she is doing.*)

DAVE: Now I will give you speech. (*He draws something unseen from his mouth and throws it to DANNY, then he kisses his finger and places the kiss on ADA's lips.*) Tell me, what does it feel like to be a human being?

DANNY (*in his gruff voice*): It's a little strange. But I'm getting used to it. It's very exciting.

(ADA *relaxes and becomes herself and involved in the questioning.*)

ADA: Now that you have eyes and tongue to see and talk and limbs to move – move, and tell me what you see.

DANNY (*in his own voice*): Hedges!

ADA: No no Daniel. That's a name, that's not what you see.

DANNY (*in his own voice from now on*): I see thin pieces of wood. Going all over the place. With bumps on them, and thin slips of green like paper, and some funny soft stuff on them.

ADA: *Now* you can use names.

DANNY: They're hedges with leaves and berries.

ADA: Any colours?

DANNY: The hedges are brown, the leaves are green and the berries are red and black.

ADA (*becoming excited*): What else can you see O Daniel?

DANNY: A blue sky with white cloud.

ADA: More?

DANNY: Birds with long necks.

ADA: More?

DANNY: Green fields with brown bumps.

ADA: More?

DANNY: A red brick house and that's where I live.

ADA: Now you are a real human being Daniel who can look and think and talk and you can come out and slay the lions.

(*We hear* DANNY *run right across the back of the stage (past barn and hedges) crying:* 'I'm coming I'm coming I'm coming!' *and* ADA *crouches down with her arms outstretched to receive him as the night and –*)

THE CURTAIN FALL[1]

[1] The boy could perhaps rush on to the stage as the lights fade. Director's decision.

ACT THREE

SCENE I

It is warm autumn. Three years have passed. 1956. The wall in front of the barn is lowered. No one works there now.

Two women are seated in the garden. CISSIE *and* ESTHER KAHN, *maiden aunts of* ADA. *The first is a trade unionist, the other owns a market stall.* CISSIE *is shelling peas.* ESTHER *is peeling potatoes.*

There is a lovely light in the sky and two deck chairs near the back door.

ESTHER: A guest house they call it.

CISSIE: Esther, stop grumbling – peel!

ESTHER: Three hundred ditches we had to jump over before we even reached the house – and they advertise in newspapers. For peace and quiet and a modest holiday – the Shambles. A very inviting name. Mind you, for a dirty week-end, this place – you know what I mean?

CISSIE (*not really minding*): Why must you be so bloody crude Esther?

ESTHER: What's the matter – all these years you been my sister and you don't know me yet?

CISSIE: What time does Dave come back for lunch?

ESTHER: One o'clock.

CISSIE: Ada'll come back from shopping with him, I suppose.

ESTHER: They better be on time else that dinner'll be burnt.

CISSIE: What?

ESTHER: Don't say 'what?', say 'ah?' Fine bloody holiday this. Only two mad maiden aunts like us would do this. Do you realize that we haven't stopped working since we've been here? Look at that job we did yesterday. Pulling up weeds. Agricultural workers!

CISSIE: Stop grumbling. You know you're enjoying yourself.

57

ESTHER: You think they make all their other guests work like this? No wonder they get so few. Cissie – I think we should tell them.

CISSIE: What?

ESTHER: Don't say 'what?', say 'ah?' We should tell them that people when they go on holiday they don't like digging gardens and feeding chickens.

CISSIE: Don't be daft woman. It's only us. We spoil her. Both her and Ronnie we spoilt.

ESTHER: A guest house they call it. Not even a bleedin' flush lavatory. Just three hundred ditches.

CISSIE: Hush Esther.

ESTHER: What's the matter for Gawd's sake? You frightened someone'll hear me? (*Shouting*) Cissie, have you stopped peaing yet?

CISSIE: So help me you're mad.

ESTHER: I'm keeping in training. Though I must say this ain't the most inspiring place for selling underwear. I mean what do their guests do here? The only sights to see are sixty clucking hens waiting to be slaughtered – poor sods – and a two-hundred-year-old barn. A historical monument!

CISSIE: That used to be Dave's workshop.

ESTHER: What did he leave it for?

CISSIE: Ada was telling me that one day about six months ago, he built a beautiful dressing table for someone and he had a lorry come to collect it, and the driver took no care on the bumpy lane so that by the time they reached the main road they'd knocked all the corners off it. A two-hundred-pound job it was, all his own design, ruined! So he found a new workshop in the village.

ESTHER: And he still can't earn money. Poor sod. He works hard that one – and what for? For peanuts that's what for!

CISSIE: Well today may change all that.

ESTHER: You mean the loan?

CISSIE (*nodding*): If he's managed to persuade the bank to loan him money he can buy machinery and his work'll be easier.

ESTHER: Now *that's* something I don't understand. I can remember him saying when he first moved here that he wanted to make furniture with his own hands. Now he's buying machinery, he'll be like a factory only not big enough to make their turnover. So where's the ideals gone all of a sudden?

CISSIE: Esther, you're a stall-owner, you don't understand these things.

ESTHER: All right, so I'm a coarse stall-owner. I'm a silly cow. So *I'm* a silly cow and *you're* a clever trade union organizer – you explain it to me.

CISSIE: It's all got to do with the work of another socialist furniture-maker, William Morris.

ESTHER: A yiddisha fellow?

CISSIE: He was a famous person. He used to say 'Machines are all right to relieve dull and dreary work, but man must not become a slave to them.'

ESTHER: So?

CISSIE: So Ada says Dave says if he can buy a machine to saw the wood, and another to plane it, that will save him a lot of unnecessary labour and he can still be a craftsman.

ESTHER: I'll tell you something Cissie! Our nieces and nephews are all mad. Look at Ronnie – working in a kitchen, and that silly arse has fallen in love with a waitress.

CISSIE: So what's wrong with a waitress? Beatie Bryant's a very nice girl, very active, bless her.

ESTHER: I know she's a nice girl but she doesn't know what Ronnie's saying half the time.

CISSIE: If it comes to that neither do I. You know where she comes from? About twenty miles from here. Ronnie met her when he came to work in Norwich.

(CISSIE *rises and enters kitchen to put peas in pot.* ESTHER *follows.*)

ESTHER: Another wandering Jew. Another one can't settle himself. Hopping about all over the country from one job to another. I'll tell you something Cissie – it's not a joke. Ronnie worries me. He worries me because his father was just the same. You know Harry? Before he fell ill! The way he couldn't stick at one job? The same thing! All over again. It worries me.

CISSIE: Now Esther don't you ever tell him that – you hear me?

ESTHER: Me? I wouldn't say a word! But it worries me. And he wants to spread socialism. Everybody's busy with socialism. 'Aunty Esther' he says 'I've finished making speeches, I'm going to marry a simple girl and hand it all on to her.' So I says to him 'Ronnie' I says 'be careful. Don't hand it on to her *before* you're married.' The meat! (*Turns to oven.*)

(*At this point* ADA *and* DAVE *appear.*)

ADA: What's happened to Aunty Esther?

CISSIE: It's all right darling, she's just gone to look at the meat. She always rushes like that – as if the world was on fire. – What's the matter Simmonds? You look all done in.

DAVE: Bank managers. How do you talk to them?

CISSIE: Like I talk to employers when I'm negotiating a strike – as though you're doing them a favour by coming at all.

ESTHER (*coming out of the kitchen*): Fifteen more minutes and we can eat.

ADA: You're bricks, the pair of you.

ESTHER: You mean we got thick skulls?

CISSIE: Stop grumbling.

ESTHER: All she can say to me is 'Esther stop grumbling.' I'm a happy woman, let me grumble. So tell us, what happened? (*Returns to chair in garden.*)

CISSIE: Wait a minute, let me get my knitting. (*Goes to kitchen.*)

ESTHER: Can't you ever sit still and do nothing?

CISSIE: No I bloody can't. The good Lord gave me hands and I like using them.

ESTHER: The good Lord gave you an arse but you don't have to be sh . . .

CISSIE: *Esther!*

ESTHER: She's so squeamish your aunt.

CISSIE (*returning and sitting on deck chair*): Right, now let's hear what happened – I'm very interested.

ADA: I must go in and lay the table, I can hear from inside. (*DAVE moves to the barn and cleans some of his tools.*)

ESTHER: What's the matter with everybody? No one can sit still for five minutes. This one knits, this one must lay the table, that one mucks about with his tools –

CISSIE: He's cleaning his chisels, Esther.

ESTHER: Don't split hairs with me. It's a bleedin' conspiracy to make me feel guilty – well nuts to yers all, I'm sitting still. I'm a lady. A bleedin' civilized lady on holiday. Fan me somebody!

CISSIE: Esther, maybe the kids don't feel like joking.

ESTHER: Dave Simmonds, are you going to tell us what happened at the bank or not?

DAVE: Nothing much. He said I could have an overdraft of two hundred pounds but no loan.

ESTHER: So what you feeling unhappy for? With an overdraft you can lay down deposit on two machines and pay off over three or five years. Who buys anything outright these days anyway.

DAVE: Yeah.

CISSIE: Hey Addie – what kind of school dinners does Danny get?

ESTHER: A real grasshopper mind you've got. Can't you stick to one subject at a time?

CISSIE: Leave off Esther, can't you see the boy doesn't want to talk about it.

(ADA *comes out of the kitchen. She is rubbing her hands and face on a towel very slowly. Although she looks red-eyed from washing, she really has been crying and is covering up with a wash.*)

ADA: They're not bad. A little bit dull but he gets plenty of it.

ESTHER: Have you been crying Ada?

CISSIE: Leave off Esther, I tell you.

ESTHER: For crying out loud what's been happening to you two?

(DAVE *looks up and sees that, in fact,* ADA *has been crying. He lays down his saw, approaches her, and takes her in his arms. After a bewildered moment of looking at them and each other –*)

CISSIE and ⎱ (*between them*). Ah Ada darling. My pet. Sweet-
ESTHER ⎰ heart. Don't cry love. Ah there poppit, what is it then?

(*Both aunts start fussing the couple but are unable to do anything except commiserate and get in each other's way while moving around trying to get in somewhere. They cannot reach either of the two.* DAVE *and* ADA *stand locked together and rocking, their own misery being the centre of the aunts' faintly comic and frustrated concern.*)

CISSIE (*having tripped over* ESTHER's *feet*): Get back to your deck chair, I'll handle this.

ESTHER: Cissie, carry on knitting and leave off. You always were heavy-handed with people.

CISSIE: That's how it should be. As soon as *you* start handling people you have them in tears.

ESTHER: And you treat every upset as though it was an industrial dispute.

ADA: Listen to those two. Anyone would think we were still fifteen.

DAVE: Feeling better sweetheart?

ADA: How can anyone feel depressed with those two old hens clucking round you.

ESTHER: Here, let me tell you about the time Ronnie made a supper of rice.

CISSIE: That's it, tell them about the time Ronnie made us a supper of rice.

DAVE: Listen to them darling, don't they sound like a music-hall act?

CISSIE: Ronnie invites himself to supper and says he wants to try out a special pork curry –

ESTHER: A very kosher dish he assures us –

CISSIE: We don't even like curry –

ESTHER: Never mind, we agree. What a mess! A whole pound of rice he puts into a saucepan and he starts to boil it – so you know what happens when you boil rice –

CISSIE: It swells!

ESTHER: The whole pound of rice began to swell. And what does he do when it reaches the top of the saucepan? He puts half of it in another saucepan and sets them both to boil. And do you think it was cooked?

CISSIE: Of course it wasn't! And the two saucepans got full again – so he gets two more saucepans and halves them again. For two hours before we got home he was cooking rice –

ESTHER: And by the time we arrived he had five saucepans and two frying pans filled with rice for a supper of three people.

(*Everyone is in a paroxysm of laughter until, as they emerge out of it,* ESTHER *suddenly remembers –*)

ESTHER: Oh yes – there's some mail for you.

DAVE: Thank God – at last!

ESTHER: At last, what?

CISSIE: We thought all you wanted was a loan.

ADA: You have to have people to buy the furniture as well you know.

CISSIE: And there's no people?

ADA: Some, but it's mostly for window sashes.

ESTHER: What's so important with the letter then?

DAVE: The letter is important because three weeks ago I had an inquiry for an originally designed suite of dining-room chairs and table and I sent in an estimate and this should be a reply. If they don't want it, it means I have to carry on doing window sashes.

ESTHER: And what's Ada crying for?

DAVE: She's having a baby.

(*Cries of joy and surprise and 'muzzeltov' and more fussing from the aunts.*)

ESTHER: So what's there to cry about? Are you sure?

ADA: Of course I'm sure you silly bitch.

ESTHER: Right, then if you don't mind I'm going to say something.

DAVE: Esther, I think we're going to mind –

ESTHER: I'm still going to say it.

ADA: Aunts, please, we're really very tired.

ESTHER: For Gawd's sake! It's not as though we're strangers. We're your aunts. All your life, till we die.

DAVE: What are you going to tell us? We're mad to stay here? Everyone's told us this. Half our battle here has been against people who for a dozen different reasons have tried to tell us we're mad.

ESTHER: Never mind about madness – but you've changed. You're not the same. Once upon a time we could talk to you. You got troubles? So tell us. What's the matter – you think we're going to laugh?

DAVE: We're tired Esther, leave us alone, yes?

ESTHER: Nice life! Lovely! It's a great pleasure knowing you! Open the letter.

DAVE: I *know* what's in the letter. Dear Mr Simmonds, after having carefully considered your designs and estimate we feel sorry to have to inform you – God! I'm learning to hate people!

ESTHER (*telling a story*): My mother loved her children. You know how I know? The way she used to cook our food. With songs. She used to hum and feed us. Sing and dress us. Coo and scold us. You could tell she loved us from the way she did things for us. You want to be a craftsman? Love us. You want to give us beautiful things? Talk to us. You think Cissie and I fight? You're wrong silly boy. She talks to me. I used to be able to watch everything on television, but she moaned so much I can't even enjoy rubbish any more. She drives me mad with her talk.

DAVE: I talked enough! You bloody Kahns you! You all talk. Sarah, Ronnie, all of you. I talked enough! I wanted to do something. Hands I've got – you see them? I wanted to do something.

ESTHER: Hands is the only thing? I'm a worker too. Haven't I worked? From selling flags at a football match to selling foam cushions in Aylesbury market. From six in the morning till six at night. From pitch to pitch, all hours, all my life! That's not work? It doesn't entitle me to a house? Or a fridge? I shouldn't buy a washing machine? How do you *measure* achievement for Christ's sake? Flower and Dean Street was a prison with iron railings, you remember? And my one ambition was to break away from that prison. 'Buy your flags' I used to yell. 'Rattles at rattling good prices' I used to try to be funny. So I sold rattles and now I've got a house. And if I'd've been pretty I'd've had a husband and children as well and they'd've got pleasure from me. Did money change me? You remember me, tell me, have I changed? I'm still the same Esther Kahn. I got no airs. No airs me. I still say the wrong things and nobody

minds me. Look at me – you don't like me or something?
That's all that matters. Or no, not that, not even like or
dislike – do I harm you? Do I offend you? Is there something about me that offends you?

DAVE (*simply*): You haven't got a vision Esther.

ESTHER: A prophet he is!

DAVE: No! We should turn to *you* for prophecies! With your
twopenny halfpenny flags and your foam cushions? With
your cheap jewels, your market lies, and your jerry houses?

ADA: Dave, sweetheart – there's no point – you'll only upset
yourselves – and she doesn't mean –

DAVE: No, no. She can take it. Straight Jane and no nonsense
she says. Let's talk back a little. I know we decided not to
bother to explain but I'm fed up being on the receiving
end. I'll tell them. (*To* ESTHER) Once and for all I'll tell
you – you call me a prophet and laugh do you? Well, I'll
tell you. I *am* a prophet. Me. No one's ever heard of me
and no one wants to buy my furniture but I'm a bleedin'
prophet and don't anyone forget that. As little as you see
me so big I am. Now you look at me. I picked up my
spear and I've stuck it deep. Prophet Dave Simmonds, me.
With a chisel. Dave Simmonds and Jesus Christ. Two
yiddisha boys –

ESTHER: Hatred, Cissie. Look at our nephew-in-law, hatred in
every spit.

DAVE: Well, what have you left me for God's sake? You
want an angel in me? Ten years I spent here trying to
carve out a satisfactory life for my wife and kids and on
every side we've had opposition. From the cynics, the
locals, the family. Everyone was choking with their experience of life and wanted to hand it on. Who came forward
with a word of encouragement? Who said we maybe had
a little guts? Who offered one tiny word of praise?

ESTHER: Praise pretty boy.

DAVE: Yes, praise! It would hurt you, any of you? There isn't enough generosity to spare a little pat on the back? You think we're cranks – recluses? Well, I'll surprise you, look – no long hair, no sandals. Just flesh and blood. Of course we need a little praise. (*Dips in his pocket for coins.*) Or maybe you want me to buy it from you! Like in the market! Here, two half-crowns for a half-minute of praise. I'll buy it! You can't afford to give it away? I'll pay for it! Five bob for a few kind words, saying we're not mad. Here y'are – take it! Take it!

CISSIE: There! You satisfied Esther? Now you've upset him, you happy?

ESTHER (*subdued*): I know, I know. I'm just a silly old cow. You want to build Jerusalem? Build it! Only maybe we wanted to share it with you. Now open the letter.

(DAVE *opens the letter, but before he has had a chance to look at it the curtain comes down so that we do not know what it says.*)

SCENE 2

Three years later. 1959.

The Simmondses are moving out. SARAH *and* RONNIE *are there helping them. Everyone is that much older.*

SARAH *is sweeping up the kitchen.* ADA *is attending to a third baby, who is in a carry-cot up stage.* DAVE *is just taking a box off stage to where the removal lorry is waiting.* RONNIE *is beside a pile of books that are waiting to be packed away.*

But at this moment they are all listening to the radio.[1]

ANNOUNCER: Captain Davies, Conservative, 20,429. J. R. Dalton, Labour, 10,526. L. Shaftesbury, Liberal, 4,291.

[1] Alternatively, the words given here as a radio announcement could be read out by Ronnie from a newspaper, in which case instead of switching off the radio at the end of the announcement Ronnie would crumple up the newspaper.

Conservative majority 9,903. The Liberal candidate forfeits his deposit. These latest results bring the Conservative majority up to 93 and will ensure the return to power in the House of Commons of the Conservative Party for a third time in succession since the end of the war. Mr Gaitskell went to Transport House this morning to confer with other Labour leaders – he looked very tired –

RONNIE (*switching off*): Well – you've chosen the right time to return anyway. You came in with them and you go out with them – whisht. (*Continues looking through books in silence.*) I'm all washed up. I don't know why the hell you asked me to help with this morbid job.

ADA: Go home then dear boy.

DAVE (*returning with an empty tea chest*): Here's the box to put the books in.

RONNIE: I said I'm all washed up. I'm complaining. (*No response.*) No one listens to me now. Funny that, everybody loo-ves me but nobody listens to me. Everyone thinks what I say doesn't count. Like they used to think of Dad. Poor old Harry – poor old Ronnie. But you forgive me my trespasses don't you Addie? Look at my sister, she's still beautiful.

DAVE: It was good of you to help us cocker.

RONNIE: *That's* all I ever get away with – gestures. You give someone a hand and they think you're a saint. Saint Ronnie Kahn.

(*All continue with their respective jobs. The removal is in its last stages.* DAVE *is going round picking up stray tools to place in a tool box.* RONNIE *sings to himself.*)

RONNIE:

Come O my love and fare ye well,
Come O my love and fare ye well,
You slighted me but I wish you well.
The winter is gone and the leaves turn green,

The winter is gone and the leaves turn green,
Your innocent face I wish I never had seen.

You realize you two that having come with explanations
you must leave with explanations.

ADA: Is anyone going to care that much Ronnie?

RONNIE: Yes, me! Jesus, one of us has got to make a success of
something. You can understand the Labour Party losing
the elections again, they change their politics like a suit
of clothing or something, but us – well you two, you
put it into practice, God knows why you lost.

ADA: Let's forget it Ronnie.

RONNIE (*jumping up*): No, don't let's forget it. You can still
change your mind. Let's unpack it all. Pay the removers
and try again. There must be something –

DAVE: Don't go on Ronnie, I keep telling you.

RONNIE: But you can't just pack up –

DAVE: I said shut up!

RONNIE:

The rope is hung and the noose hangs high
The rope is hung and the noose hangs high
An innocent man you have all sent to die.

SARAH: What is it, a funeral here?

DAVE: Any chance of a last cup of tea before we go Mum?

SARAH: Tea I can always make.

RONNIE: Tea she can always make.

There ain't a lady livin' in the land
What makes tea like my dear old mum –
No there ain't a lady livin' in the land
What –

What rhymes with 'mum'?

SARAH: Everything he makes into a joke.

DAVE: Did you ever hear what happened to Beatie Bryant,
Ronnie?

69

RONNIE: No.

DAVE: The girl you wanted to change.

RONNIE: Change! Huh! You know what my father once said to me? 'You can't change people Ronnie' he said, 'you can only give them some love and hope they'll take it.' Well Beatie Bryant took it but nothing seemed to happen.

DAVE: Three years is a long time to go with a girl.

RONNIE: I don't regret it. Maybe something did happen. After all little Sarah, wasn't it you who was always telling us that you don't know people without something happening?

SARAH: I'm always telling you you can't change the world on your own – only no one listens to me.

RONNIE: We carry bits and pieces of each other, like shrapnel from a war. Ada's like you Sarah, strong! I'm charming, like my father, and weak. O God! Isn't it all terribly, terribly sad. (*Suddenly*) Let's do an Israeli dance before we go – come on, let's dance. (*Starts doing a Zanny Hora on his own.*) The wandering Jews move on – bless 'em. Let there be music, let there be –

ADA: Stop clowning Ronnie, we won't be done in time.

RONNIE: Don't argue! Don't sing! Don't clown!

ADA: You don't have to do anything.

RONNIE: That's right. I don't *have* to do anything – except pack up and go home. We're none of us what you could call 'returning heroes' are we? If only we could squeeze a tiny victory out of it all. God, there must be a small victory somewhere for one of us. Maybe I was a good son eh? Before he died I used to wash Harry and shave him. It took him too long to walk so I used to carry him in my arms, like a cooing baby. Then I'd bounce him on the bed and play with him and he used to laugh, a really full laugh. Funny that, in the last months he couldn't talk but his laughter was full. Mummy even used to try to play cards with him but he couldn't hold them. Sometimes I laid *my* head in *his* arms to make him feel he could still – (*It is too painful to continue.*) No – I don't have to do anything. Only the old worthies are left biding their time, waiting for the new generation. Look at old Mother there, like a patient old tigress – she's still waiting. Nothing surprised you did it Sarah? You still think it'll come, the great millennium?

SARAH: And you don't?

RONNIE: Well, I haven't brought it about – and they (*of* ADA *and* DAVE) haven't brought it about, and the Monty Blatts and Cissie and Esther Kahns haven't brought it about. But then Dad said it would never happen in our lifetime – 'It'll purify itself' he used to say. The difference between capitalism and socialism he used to say was that capitalism contained the seeds of its own destruction but socialism contained the seeds of its own purification. Maybe that's the victory – maybe by coming here you've purified yourselves, like Jesus in the wilderness. Yes? No? (*No response. Places last three books in box, reading titles out like a list of the dead and softly kissing each one.*) *Mother* by Maxim Gorky. *My Son My Son* by Howard Spring. *Madame Bovary* by Gustave Flaubert. Lovely sound that – Flaubert. Ronnie de Flaubert.

DAVE: Did you ever finish your novel?

RONNIE: No.

DAVE: You've grown older in these last years, haven't you mate?

RONNIE: Yes.

ADA: I don't think there's anything more to pack away.

RONNIE (*making it up*):
      Pull down the blind, put away the stars,
      The lovers have left their fond house for the town,
      No more leaves will be gathered again
      And the last nightingales have gone.

ADA: Come on darling – put away your books and poems and let's be having you.

RONNIE: *You're* still smiling anyway.

ADA: Well, we shall be back for the summer holidays.

DAVE: Anyone would think it's your experiment that failed, you with your long face.

RONNIE: O my God, how near the knuckle that is.

SARAH: Come and have some tea and stop depressing each other.

RONNIE: And Mother says little. Quietly packs and takes her children home with her.

SARAH: I've been lonely for long enough Ronnie. A few more years and I'll be dead. I'm committing no crimes.

RONNIE: I never know whether to say at this point (*melo-dramatically*) 'we're all lonely' or not. As soon as I say something, somehow I don't believe it. Don't you find that with things? As soon as you pronounce something it doesn't seem true?

(*A cry of* 'Any more' *comes from off stage.*)

DAVE: The removal men are waiting. Right! Just this last case. Come on Ronnie. The rest of the stuff we'll leave for the holidays.

RONNIE: The radio too?

DAVE: No, bring the radio.

(RONNIE *and* DAVE *pick up packing-case and go off.*)

ADA: Let's make it quick Dave, because Danny and Jake'll be waiting up for us. (*To* SARAH) I wonder how the children'll take to London?

SARAH: Are you sure Aunty Esther met them at the station?

ADA: Yes, we had a telegram.

(RONNIE *and* DAVE *return.*)

RONNIE (*trying to be cheerful*): Righto me hearties. The cheerful side. Let's look at the rainbow. The silver lining. Because

72

remember – in the words of that immortal American prophet – (*Does an Al Jolson act.*)

> When April showers may come your way
> They bring the flowers that bloom in May,
> So when it's raining have no regrets
> Because it isn't raining rain you know it's ...

(*Gives up.*) ... etcetera, etcetera, et bloody cetera!

DAVE: I've found a basement workshop in London and I'll set up shop there.

RONNIE (*sadly*): A basement! The man who started work singing 'Linden Lea' in the open air returns to a basement.

ADA (*after a silence*): The sun is setting Dave. We really must be moving.

DAVE (*picking up again*): Who knows, maybe people will buy furniture in town. They say you can sell them anything in London.

ADA: We've found a house – a roof over our heads.

RONNIE (*jumping on crate*): Oh bloody marvellous!

> We've got sixpence, jolly jolly sixpence
> Di dum dee da to last us all our life
> Pom-pom to lend
> And pom-pom to spend
> And pom-pom to take home to our wives
> *Hallelujah!*

ADA (*finally unnerved*): Ronnie!

DAVE (*after a second*): I can't make you out cock. Not at all I can't make you out.

RONNIE: I'm crying Dave, I'm bloody crying.
(*Everyone is unnerved. Everyone is feeling the reality of leaving. A long pained silence.*)

DAVE: So? We're all crying. But what do you want of us. Miracles?

SARAH: I don't know what's happened to you all. Suddenly

73

you're talking and then you're shouting and then you're crying. Suddenly you start hitting each other with words.

DAVE: Well, why must he put us on pedestals.

SARAH: You were the God that fought in Spain, Dave, remember?

DAVE (*to* RONNIE): Is that it? (*Pause.*) You can't really forgive me because I didn't speak heroically about Spain, can you?

RONNIE (*reflectively*): The war that was every man's war.

DAVE: A useless, useless bloody war because Hitler still made it, didn't he, eh? And out went six million Jews in little puffs of smoke. Am I expected to live in the glory of the nineteen thirties all my life?

SARAH: Sick! ... You're all sick or something. We won the last war didn't we? You forgotten that? We put a Labour Party in power and ...

RONNIE (*with irony*): Oh, yes, that's right! We put a Labour Party in power. Glory! Hurrah! It wasn't such a useless war after all, was it, Mother? But what did the bleeders do, eh? They sang the Red Flag in Parliament and then started building atom bombs. Lunatics! Raving lunatics! And a whole generation of us laid down our arms and retreated into ourselves, a whole generation! But you two. I don't understand what happened to you two. I used to watch you and boast about you. Well, thank God, I thought, it works! But look at us now, now it's all of us.

SARAH: Did you expect the world to suddenly focus on them and say 'Ah, socialism is beautiful,' did you, silly boy? Since when did we preach this sort of poverty?

ADA (*turning on* SARAH): We were never poor! (*Softer to* RONNIE, *putting an arm round him.*) You want reassuring sweetheart? I'll reassure you, shall I? Remember what you said about carrying bits and pieces of each other? Well it's true. ...

RONNIE: The justifications!

ADA: Will you shut up and listen to me for Christ's sake? The kind of life we lived couldn't be a whole philosophy, could it?

RONNIE: Did it have to be?

ADA: Exactly! Did it have to be. Any more than your life with Beatie Bryant or Sarah's life with Harry. Whose life was ever a complete statement? But they're going to have to turn to us in the end, they're going to . . .

RONNIE: Are you mad? To us?

ADA: Us! Us! Because *we* do the living. We *do* the living. (*Pause.*)

DAVE: What do you think I am, Ronnie? You think I'm an artist's craftsman? Nothing of that sort. A designer? Not even that. Designers are ten a penny. I don't mind Ronnie – believe me I don't. (*But he does.*) I've reached the point where I can face the fact that I'm not a prophet. Once I had – I don't know – a – a moment of vision, and I yelled at your Aunty Esther that I was a prophet. A prophet! Poor woman, I don't think she understood. All I meant was I was a sort of spokesman. That's all. But it passed. Look, I'm a bright boy. There aren't many flies on me and when I was younger I was even brighter. I was interested and alive to everything, history, anthropology, philosophy, architecture – I had ideas. But not now. Not now Ronnie. I don't know – it's sort of sad this what I'm saying, it's a sad time for both of us – Ada and me – sad, yet – you knew – it's not all that sad. We came here, we worked hard, we've loved every minute of it and we're still young. Did you expect anything else? You wanted us to grow to be giants, didn't you? The mighty artist craftsman! Well, now the only things that seem to matter to me are the day-to-day problems of my wife, my kids and my work. Face it – as an essential member of society I don't really count. I'm not saying I'm useless, but machinery and modern techniques have come about to make me the odd man out. Here I've been, comrade citizen, presenting my offerings and the world's rejected them. I don't count, Ronnie, and if I'm not sad about it you mustn't be either. Maybe Sarah's right, maybe you can't build on your own.

RONNIE: Remember your phrase about people choking with their own experience?

DAVE: I remember a lot of things – come on, let's go.

RONNIE: That was your apology for defeat, was it?

DAVE (*wearily*): All right, so I'm defeated. Come on, let's go –

RONNIE (*desperately*): Then where do we look for our new vision?

DAVE (*angrily*): *Don't* moan at me about visions. Don't you know they don't work? You child you – visions don't work.

RONNIE (*desperately*): They *do* work! And even if they don't work then for God's sake let's try and behave as though they do – or else nothing will work.

DAVE: Then nothing will work.

RONNIE (*too hastily*): That's cowardice!

DAVE: *You* call me a coward? You? I know your kind, you go around the world crooning about brotherhood and yet you can't even see a sordid love affair through to the end. I know your bloody kind.

ADA: Dave! This is so silly –

DAVE: Well, I've tried haven't I? Everybody wants explanations and I've tried. Do you think I want to go?

RONNIE: It wasn't sordid, you know Dave. I know I didn't see it through to the end but it wasn't sordid. Beatie Bryant could have been a poem – I gave her words – maybe she became one. But you're right. There isn't anything I've seen through to the end – maybe that's

76

why you two were so important to me. Isn't that curious?
I say all the right things, I think all the right things, but
somewhere, some bloody where I fail as a human being.
Like my father – just like poor old Harry. O Christ!
Look at me.

(RONNIE *sinks to his knees in utter despair.*
They stand and watch him a while.
ADA *moves to him, but* DAVE *holds her back.*
SARAH *is about to move to him but* DAVE *stops her with*
'Sarah!'
RONNIE *is to receive no more comfort. No one can help him*
now but himself.
Slowly, very slowly, he unfolds and they all watch him.
Slowly, very slowly, he rises to his feet. He knows what is
wanted of him but still cannot do more than stand in a sort of
daze, looking from one to another – then –)

DAVE (*to* ADA): Darling, did you post those letters off?

ADA (*she understands that they must indicate that they are going on*):
Yes, Dave, and the estimates went off too.

DAVE: Where did you put the drawings?

ADA (*indicating brief-case*): It's all right, they're here. All those
you've decided to keep I've rolled up into one pile. The
rejects I burned last night.

DAVE: Now don't forget, first thing tomorrow morning I
must get in touch with the electricians and tell them to
start wiring the place up. Then there's that appointment
with Mrs What's-her-name for her bloody awful wardrobe.

(ADA *goes over to pick up the carry-cot.*)

ADA: When we've finished unpacking tonight we'll make a
list of all the things we must do – just before we go to
bed. (*She and* DAVE *pick up cot.*) Come on Simmonds
number three, we'll soon be back again for your holidays,
you can still grow up here, yes you can, or won't *you* care?

DAVE: Ronnie – lock up and stick the key in your pocket, there's a good lad. Sarah, you take your daughter's bags, God knows what she's got in them.

(DAVE *picks up his brief-case and he and* ADA *go off with the carry-cot, still talking.*)

ADA: Are you sure you turned the calor gas off properly?

DAVE: Positive. Now look darling – you mustn't let me forget to phone those electricians – Hey! Did we pack my drawing boards away?

ADA: Yes, yes, Simmonds. In those first boxes, don't you remember?

DAVE: Funny, I don't remember . . .

ADA (*to* SARAH *and* RONNIE): Come on, you two, the men are waiting.

(*They have gone off by now.* RONNIE *has locked the door and* SARAH *is waiting for him. He takes one of the baskets from her and puts an arm on her shoulder.*)

RONNIE: Well Sarah – your children are coming home now.

SARAH: You finished crying, you fool you?

RONNIE: Cry? We must be bloody mad to cry, Mother.

(SARAH *goes off leaving* RONNIE *to linger and glance once more around. Suddenly his eye catches a stone, which he picks up and throws high into the air. He watches, and waits till it falls. Then he cups his hands to his mouth and yells to the sky with bitterness and some venom –*)

RONNIE: We – must – be – bloody – mad – to cry!

(*The stage is empty.*
Soon we hear the sound of the lorry revving up and moving off. A last silence.
Then –)

A LAST SLOW CURTAIN

HOOLYIT HOOLYIT

1. Hool-yit hool-yit baiz-a vin-ten Yetzt iss ei-er
2. Brent a licht-el er-getzt toon-kle Lesht mit tzor-en

tseit Long vet dor-en noch de-er vin-ter
aus Rize die sho-ben fon d-ie lut-ten

Zu-mer i-is no-och vi-ite Long vet dor-en
Fen-ster ri-ist a - rau-aus Rize die sho-ben

noch de-er vin-ter Zu-mer i-is no-och vite.
fon d-ie lut-ten Fen-ster ri-ist a - raus.

COME OH MY LOVE

Old American Folk Song